# CROPS
## in POTS

# CROPS in POTS

How to **Plan, Plant,** and **Grow Vegetables, Fruits,** and **Herbs** in **Easy-Care Containers**

BOB PURNELL

Photography by FREIA TURLAND

Reader's Digest

The Reader's Digest Association, Inc.
Pleasantville, New York/Montreal

A READER'S DIGEST BOOK

This edition published by The Reader's Digest Association, Inc., by arrangement with Octopus Publishing Group Limited

Copyright © Octopus Publishing Group Ltd. 2007

FOR OCTOPUS PUBLISHING GROUP LIMITED
Executive Editor: Sarah Ford
Managing Editor: Clare Churly
Executive Art Editor: Karen Sawyer
Designer: Miranda Harvey
Senior Production Controller: Martin Croshaw

FOR READER'S DIGEST
U.S. Project Editor: Mary Connell
Canadian Project Editor: Pamela Johnson
Canadian Consulting Editor: Trevor Cole
Project Designer: Mabel Zorzano
Associate Art Director: George McKeon
Executive Editor, Trade Publishing: Dolores York
Associate Publisher: Rosanne McManus
President and Publisher, Trade Publishing:
  Harold Clarke

Library of Congress Cataloging in Publication Data:
Purnell, Bob.
    Crops in pots : how to plan, plant, and grow vegetables, fruits, and herbs in easy care containers / Bob Purnell.
      p. cm.
    Includes index.
      ISBN-13: 978-0-7621-0842-8
      ISBN-10: 0-7621-0842-8
    1. Container gardening. 2 Vegetable gardening. 3. Fruit-culture. 4. Herb gardening. I. Title.
      SB418.P88 2006
      635.9'86--dc22
                        2006051458

For more Reader's Digest products and information, visit our website:
  www.rd.com (in the United States)
  www.readersdigest.ca (in Canada)

NOTE TO OUR READERS
The 50 designs in *Crops in Pots* call for hundreds of different plants. No garden center carries every species, much less every cultivar included here, so in some instances you may have to make substitutions. Carry this book with you and let a knowledgeable salesperson help select plants with both a similar appearance and cultural requirements to those in the book. When buying perennials, check to see whether they are hardy in your climate. If not, you'll need to overwinter those you want to save. Set the pots in a bright, airy spot that is cool but not freezing. Keep the soil lightly moist while the days are short and gray in the winter and resume normal watering and fertilizing when the plants resume quick growth in the spring.

**Front cover (left to right):** Pepper Pot, Kale and Cabbage, Pasta and Pizza Pot, Gorgeous Grapes.
**Back cover (left to right):** An Apple a Day, Pretty in Purple, Currant Affair.
**Front flap:** Tumbling Toms.
**Half-title page (left to right):** Sunny Show, Tea Pot, Gorgeous Grapes, Pear Delight.
**Title page (left to right):** Currant Affair, A Taste of the Mediterranean, An Apple a Day, Ornamental Onions.
**At right (top to bottom):** Gorgeous Gourds, Lettuce and Tulips, Pear Delight.

Printed in China

5 7 9 10 8 6 4

# Contents

## Getting started    6

How to use this book  8
Why grow edible plants in pots?  9
Siting and grouping containers  11
Mixing edible plants with ornamentals  12
Choosing containers  13
Choosing potting mixes  15
How to plant a pot  16
How to plant a hanging basket  17
Propagation  18
How to grow plants from seed  19
General care  20
Watering  22
Mulching  25
Fertilizing  26
Pests and diseases  27

## Starters    30

Peas in a pod  32
Cut-and-come-again  34
Super salad  36
Tumbling toms  38
Towering thymes  40
Lettuce and tulips  42
Stir-fry  44
Sunny show  46
Lettuce and lobelia  48
Summer cocktail  50
Fish lovers bouquet  52
Ornamental onions  54

## Main courses    56

Red and gold  58
Potted potager  60
Pods and cobs  62
Perfect partners  64
Floral feast  66
Select salad  68
Sky high  70
Winter vegetable cubes  72
Pasta and pizza pot  74
Once upon a time  76
Textural treats  78
Mint medley  80
On fire!  82
Potato paradise  84
Peas and beans  86
Pretty in purple  88
Roots and shoots  90
Red devil  92
Pepper pot  94
Purple and bronze  96
A taste of the Mediterranean  98
Kale and cabbage  100
On the bay  102
Fireball  104
Green garnish  106
Lots of leaves  108

## Desserts    110

An apple a day  112
Blueberry surprise  114
Lemon zest  116
Strawberry ball  118
Gorgeous grapes  120
Currant affair  122
Mellow yellow  124
Tea pot  126
Pop and go  128
Gorgeous gourds  130
Pear delight  132
Passion fashion  134

## What to grow    136

Vegetables  138
Fruits  148
Herbs  151
Edible flowers  156

Index  158
Useful resources  160
Acknowledgments  160

# Getting started

How to use this book     8

Why grow edible plants in pots?     9

Siting and grouping containers     11

Mixing edible plants with ornamentals     12

Choosing containers     13

Choosing potting mixes     15

How to plant a pot     16

How to plant a hanging basket     17

Propagation     18

How to grow plants from seed     19

General care     20

Watering     22

Mulching     25

Fertilizing     26

Pests and diseases     27

# How to use this book

This book presents 50 great ideas for growing fruit, vegetables, and herbs in containers. We've divided the book into three sections: Starters (pages 30–55), Main courses (pages 56–109), and Desserts (pages 110–135).

Each project includes a list of the plants and equipment you will need, step-by-step planting instructions, a beautiful photograph of the finished project shown at its peak, and a delicious recipe that uses one of the plants you have grown.

The availability of plant varieties changes greatly from year to year, so if you are unable to locate the exact variety given in the following pages, use one with similar attributes.

To help you get started, we've provided expert advice on everything you need to know about planting containers and hanging baskets, sowing plants from seed, watering, feeding and mulching, and dealing with pests and diseases.

Finally, the What to Grow section (pages 136–157) describes vegetables, fruits, herbs, and some edible flowers that are most likely to succeed in containers. So, if you want to try something different, you could create your own planting scheme by mixing and matching some of the plants that are discussed in this section.

---

## Key to care symbols

These care symbols are designed to let you know at a glance where to site and how to look after the plants in each project.

 **Site in full sun.** Plants in these projects require as much sun and warmth as possible in order to flourish and produce crops to their maximum potential.

 **Site in full sun or light shade.** Plants in these projects will flourish in either full sun or light shade. Avoid placing them in a particularly hot position since this may cause them to perform less well.

 **Requires plenty of watering.** Plants in these projects are particularly thirsty. They require additional watering in order for their fruits to swell and for them to sustain a good crop.

 **Requires moderate watering.** Although they need regular and thorough watering, the plants in these projects are more equipped to survive with less water, so overwatering may have a detrimental effect on some.

 **Feed regularly.** Plants in these projects are heavy feeders and should be given a regular balanced supplementary feed using a liquid or soluble fertilizer to keep them healthy and cropping well.

 **Frost hardy.** Plants in these projects are fully hardy and should survive temperatures as low as 5°F (-15°C), although not for prolonged periods. Site containers in as protected a position as possible during cold periods to prevent their roots from freezing.

 **Frost tender.** Some of the plants in these projects are frost tender and temperatures below 41°F (5°C) may cause them damage. Temperatures below freezing may kill them outright.

 **Requires extra care.** Plants in these projects can be a little temperamental and require a little extra care in order to grow well and produce a good crop.

# Why grow edible plants in pots?

It is hard to imagine a more satisfying feeling than being able to dive into a plate of food that you grew yourself. Stepping out into your garden and picking fresh ingredients for a meal is a special experience that is possible almost all year long.

With a little bit of effort, you can grow all kinds of vegetables, fruits, and herbs in large and small plant containers, window boxes, and hanging baskets. If you think you would prefer to reserve precious plant-growing space for plants with greater visual appeal, think again! Edible plants in your container garden will look just as good as other plants.

Container gardening greatly expands the variety of plants you will be able to grow. Citrus fruits are frost-tender plants that may not survive winter conditions in your area. Pot them and they'll contribute to your summer display and then you can move them to a sheltered location for the winter.

Plants that would struggle in ordinary outdoor-garden soil will thrive if you treat them to more suitable surroundings that you provide for them in containers where you can customize and monitor growing conditions. If you yearn to grow blueberries that require acidic soil and your soil is alkaline, the answer is to grow them in a container filled with an acidic potting soil.

If you would like to cultivate zucchini and cucumbers that require lots of moisture, and your soil is sandy and drains water quickly, you can add moisture-retentive soil conditioners. The opposite is true for plants that require heavy soils that drain slowly, such as elderberries.

Container gardening lets you customize potting soils and regulate optimal water and light conditions for plants, which will help your plants perform much better.

## Movable feasts

Containers can also be sited conveniently close to the house, making it easier to care for your plants. Plants in pots are often less likely to be targeted by pests and diseases. If they do get attacked, having them in containers closer to your eye level will make it easier to spot any predators or disease symptoms and take care of the problem.

Thriving in separate pots, plants requiring wildly different soil conditions can be grown harmoniously side-by-side. The possibility to arrange stunning plant partnerships is greatly broadened, since what would seem impossible in a garden border or vegetable plot can become a reality in containers where many plants can coexist in close arrangements.

By understanding specific plant requirements and caring for each accordingly, moisture-loving tomatoes can be grown in separate pots alongside drough-tolerant herbs such as thyme, rosemary, and lavender and acid-loving cranberries can be sited

**Invasive plants such as mint are often best confined to containers where they can be kept firmly under control.**

Try growing plants that require different soil conditions side by side. Here a pot of lime-loving cabbages sits next to lime-hating blueberries.

Almost any plant will grow in a container, but wherever possible choose compact or dwarf-growing cultivars.

next to lime-loving cabbage and kale. By the same token, plants that may be too vigorous for the open garden can be kept under control in pots. Mints are a classic example. Containers restrict their roots and curb their spreading habit, but with correct attention they will thrive.

## No-garden gardening

In courtyards, on roof terraces and balconies, or any paved space without garden soil, containers can solve this problem of a drab expanse. Container plants are often colorful and

A garden isn't essential. Even if you have only a balcony or roof terrace, you can still grow a tasty crop of produce in containers.

successful alternatives. They make the best possible use of space and turn a stark, sterile spot into a verdant and fruitful plant-growing area.

Growing edible plants in containers offers great flexibility and freedom. Specially shaped containers can be wedged into small or awkward areas. Containers can temporarily fill an empty space that you intend to use for some other purpose later on. Many planters are easily portable and you can move, rearrange, or regroup them as needed.

To move plants permanently situated in a garden border, you ordinarily would have to wait until they are dormant before transplanting them to a different location. You can move the same types of plants if they are in pots anywhere you like during any season you desire.

You can easily remove pots of plants that have finished producing crops and replace them with other plants "waiting in the wings." Resorting to container gardening, you'll be able to have a long succession of crops that are pleasing to the eye and palatable to your tastebuds.

# Siting and grouping containers

Among the many advantages of growing plants in containers is the possibility of cultivating species that require different soil conditions and different levels of fertilizing side by side and achieving combinations that would be totally unrealistic in the borders of your garden.

## Creating atmosphere

Containers are a great way of brightening up parts of the garden that are difficult to fill with plants, such as paved areas or very dry patches at the foot of a high hedge. They can even be used to fill temporary gaps in borders or left in position as permanent fixtures. You can either "cheat" and hide the pot among other plants or make a full-blown feature of it. Many borders can be improved in this way because the contrast of color and texture provided by a terra-cotta pot, for instance, will highlight plants growing in and around it.

Collections of pots and other containers can be arranged informally or used in a more organized fashion. A row of potted quarter-standard olives, rosemaries, or lavenders in matching pots flanking a flight of steps or symmetrically spaced around a circular or rectangular pool will create a strong formal image. Potted herbs, edible flowers, and salad greens in assorted terra-cotta containers will generate a jumbly, haphazard feel. Pots can add atmosphere to any setting, and you can achieve any mood you like by choosing the appropriate combination of plants, pots, and accessories.

## Using space

As a rule, most edible plants thrive in sunny, open positions where they can develop without being drawn toward the light and where their fruits will ripen more quickly. Most fruit and vegetables need shelter from cold winds to give them a better chance of yielding a decent crop.

Backgrounds often are as important as the pots themselves and can contribute considerably to their overall appearance. The right backdrop can make a container plant look ten times better while the wrong surroundings may completely nullify its effectiveness. Pots filled with flowers always stand out better if the background is plain and unfussy. In a similar way, variegated plants need a simple background—variegated herbs set against variegated shrubs will look messy and cluttered. Other plants, fences, walls, and screens all make great backgrounds for plants in containers. It is just a matter of matching plants to their settings and settings to plants.

Finally, using containers offers you the opportunity to site your crops near seating areas, paths, windows, doors, and other places where they can be easily appreciated and readily harvested. Stepping outside the backdoor or leaning from a window to pick a few bits and pieces to use in the evening meal makes it all worthwhile.

**By grouping several containers together you can create an attractive but flexible display that can be added to or rearranged as often as you like.**

# Mixing edible plants with ornamentals

Although the vast majority of edible plants suitable for growing in containers have their own aesthetic appeal, there is absolutely no reason why purely ornamental plants cannot be planted among them in order to achieve an even more attractive display. As a bonus, vegetables are less easily detected by the many pests that would otherwise swiftly descend upon them when they are planted among herbaceous perennials and annual flowers,

## Striking a balance

The secret of success is to strike a balance between creating a colorful, interesting display and growing a worthwhile crop. Be sparing with ornamental plants; use them to enhance rather than detract from edible components in a container.

Avoid planting vigorous ornamental varieties with slow-maturing, edible plants because they can compete for light, water, and nutrients, resulting in a poor or nonexistent crop. Always go for ornamental plants that will not interfere with the business of producing a decent crop.

Trailing half-hardy perennials are useful partners since they will fall over the sides of the container as a foil to fruiting and edible-leaved plants that are usually more upright in their growth. The appearance of fruit trees grown in tubs can be enlivened by sowing hardy annuals, such as dwarf cornflowers (*Centaurea cyanus* cultivars), at their base. Hardy annuals are generally shallow-rooted and can be sown exactly where they are

**For maximum impact, combine edible plants with colorful ornamentals.**

to flower. They will not require planting holes that would damage tree roots nor are they likely to offer undue competition for food and water as they grow.

Annual climbing plants, such as morning glory (*Ipomoea* species and cultivars), are useful for teaming up with climbing fruits and vegetables. They can, for instance, be allowed to scramble up beside runner beans or gourds to complement and increase the visual impact of those plants.

## Beneficial insects

Flowering annuals and perennials planted among food crops will attract pollinating insects that are essential for fruiting plants, as well as insects that are natural predators of aphids and other common garden pests. Certain plants will help to deter less desirable insects. Planting French marigolds (*Tagetes patula*) near tomatoes to repel whiteflies is perhaps the most obvious example. Organic gardeners adopt this practice known as companion planting as a form of pest control.

---

**Take care!**
A final word of warning. Even though parts of otherwise edible plants are poisonous, don't pair poisonous plants with edible ones. An Internet search will bring up a list of poisonous plants too numerous to mention here. It is best to avoid them.

---

# Choosing containers

Containers are available in many shapes, sizes, styles, and materials, ranging from capacious, formal, Italianate marble urns to tiny, plain terra-cotta flowerpots. Basically any object capable of holding a decent amount of growing mix and with drainage holes in the base can be used as a container. If the object is aesthetically pleasing, it will provide a more attractive overall display. When it comes to selecting containers in which to grow vegetables and fruit, the general rule is: the bigger the better. The larger the pot you provide, the greater and more successful the crop you will reap.

## Types of containers

It pays to consider a few important factors before you buy. Take into account both the container setting and the plants you intend to grow. Terra-cotta has universal appeal; it suits any plant and fits any scene. Metallic containers, on the other hand, are a little more limited in their application, are more likely to lose their appeal in the long term, and often heat excessively.

Another important issue is practicality. Tall, slender pots are elegant, but unless they are sufficiently weighed down they can be top-heavy and are likely to blow over if placed in windy locations. Where space is at a premium, such as on a roof garden or a balcony, square or rectangular pots, which can be butted together, will make the best use of space. Weight is also a major factor to consider when planning roof gardens or if you like to move your pots around regularly. In these circumstances lightweight pots made from synthetic materials are a wiser choice.

Finally, although there are plenty of bargains to be had, it pays to buy the best quality you can afford. Well-made containers usually represent better value in the long term and are an investment that, in many cases, will last a lifetime.

**Plastic** Although plastic is not one of the prettiest materials, its use is among the most practical for pots that contain vegetables and fruit; it is nonporous and any soil it contains will not dry out as quickly as with other materials. Plastic containers are also lightweight and relatively easy to move around once planted.

**Terra-cotta** These pots are manufactured in dozens of styles and shapes, from tall slender cylinders to low squat troughs and planters. The color of their clay composition will vary depending on how and where each particular pot was formed. Clay is porous and has a tendency to dry out quickly. You can minimize moisture loss by lining the inside of clay pots with plastic sheets. Also, before you purchase a terra-cotta or clay container, check to see that it is labeled as frost resistant.

**Glazed** Available in a wide range of colors, glazed clay and stoneware pots often have attractive patterns. Most glazed containers available in garden centers are rated to have a high degree of frost resistance and will last for years. Considering their long life expectancy, they are relatively inexpensive and are often available with useful matching saucers.

**Glazed pots represent good value as they are generally frostproof and so will last indefinitely.**

Metal containers are ideal for creating a modern feel but should be lined with polystyrene to insulate plant roots against extremes of temperature.

**Stone, reconstituted stone, and concrete** Natural stone containers are impressive and sculpturally beautiful and provide a distinctive air of permanence, but they are expensive. Less costly substitutes formed from reconstituted stone are a more realistic choice. Once they have been outdoors for a while, they are almost the same as the real thing.

Concrete containers have enjoyed a recent revival thanks to their no-nonsense appearance and to the range of textures and finishes that can be achieved.

Containers fashioned of stone, stone substitutes, or concrete are highly durable and frost resistant. Their biggest drawback is their weight; even the smallest pots are heavy and care should be taken to site them where they will not have to be repositioned too often.

**Terrazzo** Available in shades of gray, pink, green, and white, terrazzo containers are composed of stone chips set in resin and polished to achieve a marblelike appearance. Although not cheap, they are a cost-effective, long-lasting alternative to marble, and their clean, smooth lines make them very much at home in contemporary gardens.

**Wood** This is a material with an affinity for edible plants and also suitable for gardens in general. Custom-built wooden containers are relatively affordable and as such can be relied upon to fit an awkward space. Regular treatment with a plant-friendly wood preservative or varnish will prolong their life and a touch of colored paint will give them a completely new look.

**Metal** Modern metal containers are generally best used in contemporary settings and for simple planting schemes, although traditional lead troughs, copper pots, and galvanized buckets have been in use for centuries.

Metal containers, more than any other material will subject plant roots to extremes of temperature. On a hot summer day, in full sun, the metal will heat up considerably, possibly causing damage to delicate roots and drying out the soil. The opposite happens in winter: metal provides little insulation against frost which kills plants. Lining the inner walls with a thin sheet of plastic or bubble-wrap should ease the problem.

**Fiberglass** These containers are usually designed to imitate other more expensive materials, providing a cost-effective substitute for lead and stone. The best fiberglass pots are extremely convincing and yet are only a fraction of the price of the real thing.

Since fiberglass containers are lightweight, they are ideal for balconies and similar locations. They are weatherproof, but can be easily damaged if dropped or hit with a hard object.

**Improvised containers** Recycled and reclaimed containers test our inventiveness and imagination. Almost any stable receptacle capable of holding enough soil to sustain plant growth and in which adequate drainage holes can be made is a potential plant container.

# Choosing potting mixes

Most garden centers and nurseries offer an extensive array of growing mixes, but essentially there are just three main types (soil-based, soil-less and ericaceous mixes), all of which can be adapted as necessary to suit your plants. Never be tempted to use garden soil in place of specially prepared mixes because you will risk introducing weed seeds, pests, and even diseases. Previously used mixes may also harbor pests and diseases, so always use fresh.

## Soil-based mixes

Soil- or loam-based potting mixes are best suited to long-term plants, such as fruit trees and bushes. These mixes tend to hold moisture and nutrients for longer than soil-less mixtures do. They are also heavier and more substantial and are therefore useful in windy locations where containers might topple over. However, they do have a tendency to become hard and compacted through watering. In most cases, therefore, they are best lightened by adding a proportion of soil-less mix, perlite or another material that will improve aeration and drainage.

## Soil-less mixes

Soil-less potting mixes are composed mainly of peat or peat substitutes such as coir. They are readily available, comparatively inexpensive and, consequently, the most widely used. However, they vary enormously in quality, so it is not always wise to opt for the cheapest.

Referred to as general-purpose or all-purpose mixes, they are ideal for fast-growing plants, such as salad crops. When given extra care, however, longer-term plants will also thrive in them. Most contain sufficient nutrients for an initial period of six weeks or so, after which it is necessary to add fertilizer, either as granules or in liquid form.

Soil-less mixes are lightweight and dry out more rapidly than soil-based ones, you will need to water them more often. They can also be difficult to soak thoroughly if they are allowed to dry out.

## Ericaceous mixes

Plants such as blueberries and cranberries are intolerant of lime and require acidic rather than alkaline soils and must be planted in ericaceous or lime-free mixes in order to flourish. Planted in an ordinary mix they soon become chlorotic (the leaves turn yellow), stop thriving, and eventually die.

## Customizing mixes

By growing plants in containers you can easily cater to each plant's particular likes and dislikes. You can locate plants where they will thrive better. You can regulate watering and fertilizing protocols properly as well as tailor each plant's growing medium to its specific requirements by adding ingredients such as horticultural grit where sharp drainage is needed or water-retentive granules when high moisture conditions are important.

Incorporating inert, lightweight, and porous materials such as vermiculite and perlite will improve soil aeration. Although readily available and easy to blend into your needed soil mixture, these items are not usually included as standard ingredients in prepackaged potting soil mixes. They have an added benefit—they help make large containers more portable in situations where excessive weight is an issue.

**Clockwise from top left: Soil additives (vermiculite, perlite and horticultural grit) and mixes (soil-less, ericaceous, and soil-based).**

# How to plant a pot

The basic principles of planting a container are the same no matter what its size, shape, or material composition and no matter what plants are to live in it. Just as thorough preparation pays dividends when planting in the open ground, attention to detail and a little extra effort at the potting-up stage will result in strong, healthy growth. Make sure you have everything you will need before you begin, including clean containers.

It's good practice to wash and sterilize containers as you empty them to remove any traces of pests and diseases that might be clinging to their sides or base. If the container has been used before, empty out any old soil mix and clean the inside thoroughly. Be sure that there are adequate drainage holes in the base of your container and, if necessary, drill a few extra.

**1** Place pieces of broken terra-cotta, stones, gravel, or, if weight is a factor, chunks of polystyrene in the bottom to create a drainage layer that will help prevent waterlogging. Partly fill the container with new good-quality, soil mix adapted where necessary to suit the needs of your chosen plants. If it is dry, wet it beforehand. Soil-less mixes, especially, are difficult to re-wet once they dry out completely. Pack the soil down gently as you go and place the largest plant roughly in position to check its level. The top of its rootball should rest about 1 in. (2.5 cm) below the rim.

**2** Place all the plants while still in their original pots, in the container as a trial run. Rearrange them until you are happy with the composition. If they are dry, water them thoroughly. The tallest-growing plants should either go at the back or, if the container is to be viewed from all sides, in the center. Shorter plants and trailing varieties should be placed toward the front or the edges. Starting with the largest first, tap it out of its pot and plant it, building up the soil level as necessary. Gently tease out the roots of potbound specimens to help them establish more readily.

**3** When you are happy with the position of each plant, carefully fill around them with more soil and gently pack it down. Avoid firming too heavily, because compacted soil will not drain freely, nor be sufficiently aerated. Make sure the surface of the soil is roughly level and that there is room between it and the rim to allow for watering and, where appropriate, a layer of mulch. If the soil or mulch is level with the top of the container, it will spill over the sides when you add water.

**4** Once planting is complete, water thoroughly to settle the plants in. Be sure to direct water toward the roots. Pour slowly to allow the water to penetrate deeply and so as not to wash out any soil. Sprinkle water over the tops of the plants to clean off any splashes of soil. If necessary or desired, apply a decorative mulch as a finishing touch.

# How to plant a hanging basket

Even if you do not have or cannot spare any ground space whatsoever in your garden, you should be able to find room for one or more hanging baskets or wall planters. Selecting from dwarf runner beans to strawberries and a wide range of herbs, you'll be amazed at just what you can grow within the confines of a single basket. Choose either an open-sided, mesh-type basket that will allow you to plant through the sides as well as the top, or a solid-sided basket, the sides of which you can disguise with top-planted trailing plants, such as tumbling tomatoes.

Remember that hooks and brackets for suspending hanging baskets must be secure. A well-planted basket filled with moist soil will be very heavy. It is your responsibility to make sure that the hanging basket cannot fall and cause damage or, worse, injury.

**1** Rest the basket on an empty pot for stability and place a liner inside. In place of the traditional moss, there are plenty of materials to use including cocoa fiber, synthetic fiber liners, and wool, which can be built up in layers. If you use liners made from plastic, foam, or paper pulp, you will need to cut holes if you want to plant through the sides.

**2** To help retain moisture, place an old saucer or a small plastic plate in the bottom of the basket on top of the lining. Add a little soil mix and begin pushing plants through the holes in the sides from the inside out. At this stage it is important not to damage the roots, which will cause stunted growth.

**3** Build up the planting in the basket in two or three layers, adding more plants and mix as you go. If you wish, add water-retaining granules to the mix at this stage. Plant the top of the basket with a more upright-growing plant in the center and plants that will tumble or trail around the edges. Aim to have the level of the mix in the center of the basket to be slightly lower than that around the edges. This will help to direct water to the roots of the plants.

**4** Add controlled-release fertilizer and water thoroughly. Stand the completed basket in a sheltered place to allow the plants to establish for a couple of weeks before hanging it up in its final position.

# Propagation

One of the great added joys of growing your own food is that most of it can quite easily be raised fairly inexpensively from scratch, that is, from seed or cuttings. Once you are smitten, the pleasure and excitement you gain from raising your own plants seldom fades and are reawakened with each new batch of seedlings that germinate and every fresh cutting that roots.

## Sowing seed

Most vegetables can be raised easily from seed, especially if you have a minimum amount of equipment—notably a temperature-controlled plant rack or mini-greenhouse—necessary to provide high enough temperatures for plants such as tomatoes, peppers and eggplants to germinate. Most vegetables are so easy to raise from seed that it is hard not to be overrun with them. Most seed packets, except those of F1 hybrid seed, contain far more seeds than you'll need in a single season, so don't be tempted to sow the whole packet—unless you can handle all the resultant seedlings. As they grow on they will need increasingly more space. It is often worthwhile to team up with like-minded

---

**F1 hybrids**

The expression F1 hybrid means the first generation of plants to be derived from the crossing of two distinct, pure-bred lines. F1 hybrids come true to type, and they tend to be uniform and vigorous. F2 hybrids arise when plants from a group of F1 hybrids self-pollinate. They do not necessarily come true.

---

friends and neighbors to put together a combined seed order that can be shared equally to provide smaller quantities of a wider range of plants.

Some seed, such as that of salad crops, carrots, and beets, can be sown directly into the container, although it is often easier to nurture and protect them in the early stages by sowing them in small, individual cells of plastic seed-starter trays. These trays make transplanting easy and avoid root disturbance, which could cause stunted growth. Larger seeds, such as those of melons, cucumbers, and squashes are best sown in larger individual pots.

## Other methods

Many herbs, such as rosemary, lavender, and thyme, will root readily as cuttings, although a few, such as parsley and fennel, are best grown from seed while some others, including mints and lemon balm, can be propagated by dividing them.

Most types of fruit trees require an advanced propagating technique called grafting. Since you most likely will not want to grow a large number of any specific type of fruit tree, it's a good idea to purchase grafted specimens of whatever fruit trees you want to grow from a reputable garden center or nursery.

When you buy fruits that are soft, such as gooseberries and strawberries, make sure they are certified as virus-free stock.

---

**Substitutions**

The plant groups in this book are suggestions only. You can replace them with available plants or ones you particularly like. Some seed merchants, for example, have their own selections of cut-and-come-again lettuces and oriental greens in a range of leaf shapes and colors but you can just as easily mix seed from several different packets if you prefer to make your own combination. If you choose other plants, always bear in mind that Mediterranean herbs, such as sage and thyme, need a free-draining soil and should not be combined with plants that prefer a heavier, more moisture-retentive medium. Remember, too, that when you are including root vegetables, such as carrots, cultivars that develop a rounded shape can be grown in shallower containers than the more traditional, long carrots.

# How to grow plants from seed

Always use fresh, good-quality, seed starter mix when you are sowing seeds. These mixes generally contain less fertilizer and are less coarse than those prepared for transplanted seedlings and larger plants. Always follow the specific sowing guidelines on the seed packet, as all seeds need varying conditions and temperatures in order to germinate successfully. For instance, some seeds need light to germinate, while others will not sprout unless all light is excluded.

**1** To avoid root disturbance and the chore of pricking them out, sow seeds in cell-pack trays. These vary in size, and you should select the size that will suit the size of seed you are sowing. Very large seed can be sown into small pots 3 in. (7.5 cm) or so in diameter. Fill the pots or cells to just below the rim with a finely sieved, prepackaged seed starter mix that is moist but not too wet.

**2** Pack the mix down gently and sow fine seed, such as lettuce, that is often difficult to sow individually, in tiny pinches on the surface. Seedlings can later be thinned out if necessary. In order to sow larger seed, such as peas, beans, and cucumbers, in individual pots, use a pencil or your finger to make a hole in the center that corresponds with the sowing depth suggested on the seed packet and drop in one or two seeds. If both germinate, the weaker of the two seedlings can be discarded.

**3** Cover the seed with finely sieved mix, horticultural sand, or vermiculite. The sowing depth will vary greatly from variety to variety. Some fine seeds need light to germinate and should be simply pressed into the mix with no covering. Other relatively large seeds must be buried more deeply. After sowing, water thoroughly using a watering can with a fine sprinkler attached. Place the trays or pots into a cold frame, greenhouse, or heated plant rack, depending on the temperature required for them to germinate. Keep a close eye for signs of germination and make sure they do not dry out. At the same time, be careful not to water them too much because this can cause the seeds to rot.

**4** Once the seedlings begin to germinate, allow them maximum light but do not place them in strong, direct sunlight, which may scorch their delicate developing leaves. Frost-hardy species, such as *brassicas* and lettuce, which are often best sown outside without too much heat, can be planted in their final containers once they are large enough to handle. Tender peppers, tomatoes, and eggplants, on the other hand, must be gently acclimatized and left permanently outdoors only once all danger of frost has passed.

# General care

Apart from fertillizing and watering, most container plants will benefit from a little additional routine care as described here. Paying attention to detail will help your plants to always look their best and produce the maximum yield. A major advantage of growing plants in containers is that they are close at hand and more isolated than plants in the garden. You are more likely to notice if they are in need of attention or if they are suffering in any way.

## Avoiding pests and diseases

Ordinary hygiene and clean-up practices will cut down the risk of pests and diseases, especially among young, weak plants, which are more prone to infection. Fallen leaves and other plant debris, especially that which has been affected by pests or diseases, should be removed on a regular basis. Do not add infected plant material to a compost heap because this will only perpetuate the problem. Throw it in the trash instead.

Used containers should be thoroughly cleaned and preferably sterilized before you put new plants in them. Remember to sterilize any pruning equipment that has been used on diseased material. Wash in a 10 percent bleach solution and rinse afterwards.

## Pruning and deadheading

Many edible plants, particularly fruiting types, will benefit from pinching out, pruning, and training in order to produce compact, bushy growth and maximum crop yields. The sideshoots of vine tomatoes, for instance, should be removed as they appear, but the leading shoots of bush tomatoes may require pinching out to encourage them to bush out fully.

Remove diseased, damaged, and dying leaves on a regular basis to keep your plants looking their best and to maintain a good level of hygiene.

Misting over the open flowers of fruiting or podded plants with tepid water will help the fruits set and encourage a more bountiful crop.

Except where plants are being grown for their seed or fruits, remove faded flowers to divert their energies into producing further blooms.

Evergreen herbs grown in pots should be trimmed regularly throughout the growing season to keep their shape and ensure compact, bushy growth.

Fruit trees in containers require even more careful pruning than those in the ground to encourage the best possible crop. Apples, pears, and bush fruits are usually pruned in winter, during the plants' dormant period, although a certain amount of summer pruning may also be necessary. Stone fruits, such as cherries, plums, nectarines, and peaches, should be pruned in late spring; never do this in winter. Generally, you should adopt the same pruning regime as if the fruit trees were planted in the garden, but a little additional judicious pruning may also be required simply to keep them to a manageable size and shape.

Evergreen herbs in pots also need occasional trimming to keep them neat, and topiary specimens, such as sweet bay (*Laurus nobilis*) trained as pyramids or lollipops, should be trimmed with pruning shears a few times a year to maintain their shape.

Ornamental plants in particular should be deadheaded regularly. Keep an eye on your container plants and snip off or pick off all the flowerheads that have past their bloom. Once a plant has been allowed to set seed, it will tend to stop flowering altogether.

## Training and supporting
Many plants will need some form of support system to stop them from collapsing under the weight of a heavy crop or tossing around and toppling over in high winds. Climbing plants, such as gourds, runner beans, and passion flowers, should be trained on a wooden framework, metal obelisk, or something simpler, such as a wigwam of sticks, and then tied in regularly. This will promote even coverage and good air circulation through the center of the plants and help to avoid a messy tangle of growth. Other plants, such as bush tomatoes and dwarf beans, are also best provided with some support in the form of canes or thin sticks pushed in between them.

**Wind or tie in the stems of trailing or climbing plants, such as gourds, to prevent them becoming entangled and ungainly.**

# Watering

Plants established in the garden are largely able to fend for themselves and are free to send their roots through the soil to satisfy their "thirst" and "appetite." Plants in containers, however, cannot access moisture and nutrients beyond the confines of their pot. In effect, a plant in a container can be likened to an animal kept as a pet: It relies on its keeper for all its care. Once you understand this and begin treating your container plants accordingly, you are bound for success. You don't have to become a slave to your containers. Gardening, should be enjoyable, not a chore, and although the greater the effort you put in, the richer the rewards you'll receive, you should be able to strike a balance.

**Insert a plastic tube with small holes drilled along its length alongside thirsty plants, such as tomatoes, to make watering your containers easier.**

## Routine watering

Plants in containers will struggle on indefinitely without fertilizer, although they will perform less well and look increasingly starved. If they are deprived of water for a prolonged period, however, they will inevitably die. A dose of fast-acting fertilizer can perk up the sickliest of plants, but while even heavily wilted plants can miraculously be revived with a thorough soaking, no amount of water will resurrect a plant that has dried out and withered completely.

Rain cannot always be relied upon to water container plants because the surface of the potting mix is usually covered by a canopy of foliage that not even the heaviest downpour will penetrate sufficiently. For your plants to flourish, nutrient and water reserves must be replenished manually.

The most efficient way to water is slowly and thoroughly, using a watering can. Direct the water to the roots, not the foliage. Pour on a little and allow it to soak into the soil rather than running over the sides. Repeat the process from different sides of the pot until the entire root ball is saturated. A length of plastic pipe drilled with small holes and sunk into the pot will make sure that the water goes exactly where it is needed. This is especially useful for thirsty plants, such as tomatoes and cucumbers.

Large pots may need 2–3 gallons (9–14 liters) at a time. They will usually dry out less quickly than smaller pots, and so require watering less frequently, although the rate at which they dry out is also governed by the crops they contain.

Small pots can be placed in water-filled saucers to draw up as much moisture as they need, but most plants will resent standing permanently in water so, after a couple of hours, pour out any excess. Containers that have dried out completely can be submerged in a bucket filled with water until the soil is thoroughly soaked.

During the summer many containers may need watering twice a day, depending on their location, the weather, the moisture requirements of the individual plant and the type of

**Simple watering systems are invaluable time-savers. Drip systems are the most efficient as they direct water to the roots without any wastage.**

container. On a hot day a porous terra-cotta or clay pot in full sun will dry out noticeably faster than a glazed pot in partial shade. Watering in the cool of the morning will reduce the amount of evaporation and avoid scorching delicate leaves or developing fruits.

Most plants will forgive you the occasional missed watering, but if you are apt to forget frequently, or are simply pressed for time there are many ways of making watering easier and less time-consuming.

## Water-retaining granules

Adding water-retaining or water-storing granules to the mix at planting time can help moisture retention considerably. These swell on contact with water, holding moisture and making it available to the roots as required. They are not a substitute for proper watering but will see your plants safely through a missed watering or two.

Water-retaining granules are included in the ingredients for projects in this book when they will provide a specific advantage. However, if you find regular watering too much of a chore, you could add a small quantity to any of the projects described.

---

### Overwatering

It is possible to water too much, especially if the container does not drain freely. Waterlogging is a common problem, and the symptoms are similar to those caused by drought: wilted growth and yellowing or browning leaves that eventually drop. The only way to determine the cause of the problem is to feel the mix and increase or hold off watering as appropriate. Always make sure there are plenty of drainage holes in the base of the container and cover them with a layer of broken clay pieces to prevent them from clogging up with mix. Wherever possible, raise your containers on blocks or special plant pot feet to provide free drainage.

---

## Wetting agents

Wetting agents work slightly differently and are often included in packaged all-purpose mixes, allowing you to wet them again easily when they have dried out. Porous clay pots that dry out quickly can be lined inside with plastic to reduce moisture loss, but only line the sides, not the bottom of the container.

If you go away on vacation, try to move as many of your containers as possible to a cool spot. Grouped closely together, they will also help to shade each other.

## Watering systems

If you have a large number of containers or you go away frequently, consider investing in a simple watering system. These are inexpensive and readily available from garden centers. Although they may appear complicated at first glance, they are easy to install and adapt to your garden.

## Drip systems

Drip systems that release water slowly and efficiently are the most effective. All you have to do is turn on the water faucet and walk away before returning hours later to turn it off. Irrigation systems can also be run via a computer attached to a faucet, which can be programmed to turn on the water for a set period at a set time every day—you won't even have to be there.

## The new self-watering containers

This miraculous-sounding piece of gardening equipment is a relatively recent innovation and is becoming increasingly available through garden centers and gardening websites. When used correctly, they work extremely well, and as well as saving you a huge amount of time they invariably help to sustain a better, healthier crop. These specially-designed planters are available in a wide range of styles and sizes to suit all types of crops.

They tend to be made of plastic and are not always the most aesthetically pleasing, but you can also buy kits that allow you to turn other traditional containers into self-watering ones.

From the outside, self-watering containers appear little or no different from any other types but their internal structure is designed to provide sufficient space for potting mix and root development. A separate area in the base is designed to hold a reservoir of water. The reservoir is filled via a tube or a hole in the side of the container, which also often acts as an overflow, and the water is drawn up into the mix as needed by capillary action. In this way the mix remains consistently moist but never waterlogged. As long as the reservoir is kept replenished, your plants will never lack moisture.

The watering system can vary from one type of container to another. In most instances wicks of capillary matting are used, but others rely on a small area of the mix coming into direct contact with the reservoir. Both methods work well, and some containers employ both. A gauge is usually included that allows you to check the water level accurately. You should do that daily, if possible. The water-holding capacity will vary depending upon the size of the container, and the amount of water used in a day will also depend on weather conditions, the moisture requirements of an individual plant, and its location.

Apart from their labor-saving attributes and ease of use, a huge advantage of self-watering containers is that they draw up water from below and nutrients remain available to your plants far longer than with traditional watering methods that tend to wash (leach) nutrients out of the mix. The chore of feeding your container plants is also significantly reduced with self-watering containers.

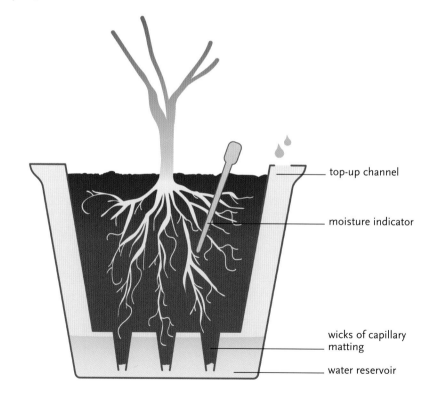

top-up channel

moisture indicator

wicks of capillary matting

water reservoir

# Mulching

Any trick that will help conserve moisture in a container is worth adopting, and mulching—covering the surface of the growing mix with a layer of loose material—is invaluable. Mulches can also be highly ornamental in addition to suppressing weeds and helping to keep roots cool and retain moisture in the mix.

## When should I use a mulch?

Mulches are not always necessary. If the surface of the mix will be quickly covered by the plants as they mature, which is often the case with fast-growing plantings, mulching is generally not necessary.

In many other cases, however, such as where fruit trees or evergreen herbs, such as sweet bay or lavender, are planted for permanent effect, a mulch applied to a depth of 2–3 in. (5–8 cm) will be highly beneficial.

Chosen to tie in with the theme of the planting or to complement the style or material of the container, mulches can considerably enhance the visual appeal of a container planting.

## Materials

A wide variety of inorganic items such as slate, pebbles, gravel, and organic matter that will slowly decompose, including chipped bark, cocoa shells, and pine cones can be used.

Slate and pebbles look particularly effective with architectural-looking plants, such as bananas or olives, especially when they are housed in terrazzo stone containers. Pine cones will enhance the appearance of pots filled with acid-loving blueberries and cranberries.

A layer of sharp grit or crushed seashells around lettuces and cabbages will deter slugs and snails. Strewn around onions and shallots, the same material will aid drainage and help to prevent rotting.

Even recycled materials, such as glass, broken tiles, and cracked clay pots, can be utilized as mulches. They can also be combined to great effect—slate with pebbles; glass with marbles; and pine cones with acorns, for example. Indeed, when it comes to being creative with mulches, you can really let your imagination run riot.

**Cocoa shells will gradually decompose so should be topped up annually.**

**A mulch of pebbles can be highly decorative and will last indefinitely.**

# Fertilizing

Most prepackaged potting mixes contain enough fertilizer to sustain your plants for only three or four weeks. After that you will have to set up a regular fertilizing schedule to supply the nutritional needs of your crop.

## Types of fertilizers

Slow-maturing crops will need a more intense fertilizing routine to sustain them than fast-maturing crops that require little or no supplementary fertilizer. Vegetables grown in pots will need more nutrients provided than they would in the open ground where nutrients and trace elements necessary for strong healthy growth are more abundant.

Various kinds of prepackaged fertilizers—some all-purpose types, others formulated for more specific applications—are available. Controlled-release fertilizers in the form of plugs that release nutrients gradually into the soil for up to six months can be placed in the container when plants are potted.

Alternatively, some potting mixes contain granules that slowly release fertilizing ingredients. These are ideal for long-term plantings such as fruit trees and bushes. Soluble or liquid fertilizers are best for fast-growing crops such as salad greens when dissolved or diluted in water and then watered into the soil.

Choose a high-potash fertilizer for flowers and fruits; for foliage, select one with high nitrogen. Some fertilizers are formulated for specific fruits or vegetables, such as high-potash fertilizers to help tomatoes flower and fruit. These are beneficial for other fruiting plants and a wide range of flowering plants as well. Citrus fruits have specific requirements and special fertilizers are available just for them.

Applying correct amounts of fertilizer regularly will result in healthier plants. Take care not to apply too much fertilizer, however, which can harm plants. Always verify the specific requirements for each crop and follow the recommended dilution and application rates listed on the packaging.

Mix up soluble fertilizers in a watering can or use a special hose attachment, following the manufacturer's recommended dosage.

Controlled or slow-release fertilizer granules can either be mixed with the soil at the potting stage or added afterwards in the form of small plugs.

# Pests and diseases

Just as in the garden itself, plants in containers can be affected by a number of pests and diseases. If possible, check every day for signs of infection because the sooner pests and diseases are detected the easier it is to eradicate them. This book describes the most common pests and diseases, but if you need more detailed information you should consult a book or the Internet.

## Common pests

**Aphids.** Aphids and other sap-sucking insects can distort a plant's growth and also transmit viral infections from plant to plant. If discovered early, they are easily controlled either by removing any affected shoots or by spraying with an organic insecticide or insecticidal soap.

**Caterpillars.** Caterpillars and larvae of a range of insects can completely devour the leaves of a plant in a matter of hours. The larvae of the cabbage white butterfly can be particularly troublesome on *brassicas*. In small numbers they can be simply be picked off by hand, but use a contact insecticide to deal with heavy infestations.

**Leafhoppers.** Leafhoppers are sap-feeding insects that live on the undersides of leaves. They cause pale, unsightly mottling of the upper leaf surface on a range of plants, including salvias and verbenas. They are tiny green insects, 1/8 in. (2–3 mm) long, with elongated bodies, and they can fly short distances—from leaf to leaf—when disturbed. Spray with a general insecticide or organic aphid control.

**Leaf miners.** Leaf miners are the larvae of insects that mine through leaf tissue, creating unsightly, straight, or meandering lines, or occasionally blotches that usually appear white or gray. Mined leaves usually dry up and die. Remove affected leaves at the first signs of attack and, if necessary, spray with insecticide.

**Spider mites.** Infestations can be identified mainly by the pale mottling and washed-out appearance of the leaves on which spider mites are feeding. They can also cause serious and unsightly damage to many outdoor container plants. They are prevalent in hot, dry conditions, and because they multiply rapidly they are difficult to control. Biological control with the tiny predatory mite *Phytoseiulus* is the most reliable combatant.

**Slugs and snails.** Slugs generally find the majority of their meals at ground level, while snails will climb in search of a tasty morsel. Growing your plants in containers gives you an advantage, but snails will eventually find them. As well as using proprietary slug baits, there are numerous other methods of control you can employ to help protect your plants. These range from attaching a ring of copper tape just under the rim of the container which gives them a slight electric shock, to sinking beer or bran traps into the ground around your pots: Slugs sipping on beer will quickly become drunk, then fall in and drown. Bran will expand inside them and cause them to explode.

**Vine weevil.** The larvae of vine weevils can cause utter devastation in containers. The tiny, off-white, brown-headed grubs spend their life eating through the roots of many container plants, which then simply collapse and die. Several effective controls have been introduced in recent years, including both biological nematodes, *Heterorhabditis megidis* or *Steinernema carpocapsae*, and chemical controls that can be watered into the soil. These controls are expensive and you will need to be persistent to eradicate these pests, but the expense and efforts are worthwhile to ensure that your favourite container plants do not succumb to these voracious pests. Although the adult weevils do not eat the roots of a plant, they do chew unsightly notches in leaves. Because they are nocturnal, they can be caught at night or provided with an upturned, straw-filled pot to hide out in by day. Check the pot regularly and destroy any weevils you find.

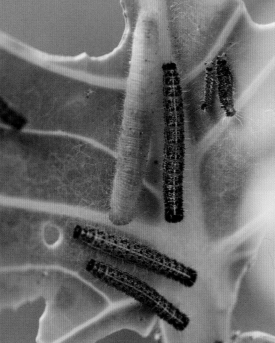
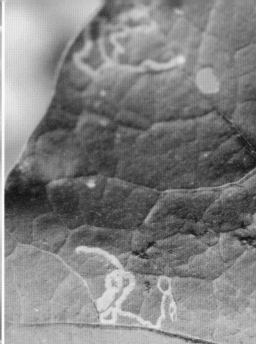

Aphids                          Caterpillars                          Leaf miner damage

**Whitefly.** Whitefly can affect outdoor plants, especially *brassicas* and tomatoes, particularly during prolonged periods of hot, dry weather, when they will breed at an astonishing rate. They are sap-feeding insects, about less than ⅛ in. (2 mm) long. Spray infested plants with pyrethrum or an insecticidal soap or use an appropriate insecticide.

**Wood lice.** Large numbers of these distinctive, nocturnal creatures, with their gray, segmented, shell-like bodies, often congregate in, under, or around containers. They are generally interested only in decaying plant material and so are not a great threat, but they can damage seedlings and will often attack leaves and stems that have already been partially devoured by slugs and snails. Remove dead leaves and decaying matter regularly from around containers to discourage them.

## Common diseases

**Blight.** This fungal disease, which attacks potatoes, tomatoes and related plants—especially *Solanum* species, is worse in wet seasons and can devastate a crop. It infects leaves, stems, and tubers. Brown patches on the leaves lead to yellowing and premature leaf fall, and in humid conditions the disease will spread rapidly. Spraying with a fungicide from early in the season will help to control the problem, but the tops of badly affected plants should be removed and destroyed.

**Grey mold (botrytis).** Botrytis is a fungus that revels in damp conditions and that manifests itself as a furry gray mold that coats leaves and stems. Removing and carefully disposing of affected plant parts, followed by an application of a general fungicide, may help prevent it from spreading, but seriously affected plants are best thrown away.

**Powdery mildew.** Powdery mildew thrives in dry conditions and shows as white spots, usually on the upper leaf surface, that gradually spread and eventually merge to coat the whole leaf. Affected leaves are unsightly and plants lose vigor. Regular and thorough watering will help prevent the problem, and spraying with baking soda (1 oz. per gallon) can also be worthwhile.

**Rust.** Rusts appear as rusty-brown pustules on the undersides of the leaves of a wide range of plants, including pelargoniums and mints. The upper surfaces of affected leaves are peppered with corresponding yellow spots. Rusts are difficult to control and are best treated as early as possible. Badly affected leaves should be removed and the rest of the plant sprayed with a

Snails                              Whitefly                            Powdery mildew

fungicide. As a rule, most types of rust are specific to a particular family or genus, so will not necessarily spread to other plants that are growing in the same container.

## Controlling pests and diseases

The fact that you are growing your own fruit and vegetables means that you have total control over whether your food is sprayed with garden chemicals. For most of us, the ideal is not to use chemicals at all but instead to employ a range of organic controls. Many gardeners would rather lose a crop than resort to chemicals, but they are available if there is no other option.

Keeping your plants healthy by watering and feeding correctly and practicing good hygiene by clearing up plant debris will cut down the risk of attack from pests and diseases. In short, prevention is better than cure.

**Chemicals.** There are a number of chemical controls, including insecticides and pesticides, aimed at curing problems on edible plants, but they really should be used as a last resort. Make sure that you always follow the manufacturer's instructions exactly and never exceed the recommended dosage. Treat chemicals with respect and use them sparingly.

**Biological controls.** Biological controls involve employing the natural enemies of a given pest and are generally effective against only that one pest, so there is no danger of harming other beneficial insects. In most cases they are far more effective in the confined environment of a greenhouse, but when correctly applied, nematodes that parasitize vine-weevil larvae and soil-dwelling slugs can be used with great success outdoors. Biological controls should never be used in conjunction with chemicals because this will kill the predator as well as the unwanted pest.

**Other organic controls.** There are many tried-and-tested methods of combating pests and diseases that do not involve using chemicals. These are loosely termed "organic controls," and their methods and applications range from using plants that deter certain pests—marigolds (*Tagetes*) repel whitefly, for instance—to setting up traps, such as upturned pots that provide cool, dark daytime abodes where slugs and adult vine weevils will congregate so that you can capture and easily dispose of them.

# Starters

Peas in a pod **32**

Cut-and-come-again **34**

Super salad **36**

Tumbling toms **38**

Towering thymes **40**

Lettuce and tulips **42**

Stir-fry **44**

Sunny show **46**

Lettuce and lobelia **48**

Summer cocktail **50**

Fish lovers bouquet **52**

Ornamental onions **54**

# Peas in a pod

Picking peas straight from the pod is twice as pleasant when you can smell the perfume of sweet peas while you do so. This simple pairing combines a diminutive pea variety with a dwarf trailing sweet pea, so both are ideal for even a fairly small container. They will tumble gently over the sides of a hanging basket and are easy to raise from seed making this an especialy rewarding project for children. Be sure to pick the sweet peas as often as possible to prolong the display.

## Ingredients

1 packet of dwarf pea seed, such as *Pisum sativum* 'Half Pint'

1 packet of dwarf sweet pea seed, such as *Lathyrus odoratus* 'Cupid' (non-edible)

biodegradable peat pots

seed-starter mix

1 willow hanging basket, 14 in. (35 cm) across

all-purpose soil-less mix

## Method

1  Sow both the peas and sweet peas individually into biodegradable peat pots filled with seed-starter mix and put them in a cold frame to germinate.

2  Select a basket, 14 in. (35 cm) across, with closed-in sides (either plastic or with a more decorative twig design) and fill with soil-less mix.

3  Plant the peas and sweet peas alternately in rings, using 6–8 plants of each to fill the basket. Deadhead the sweet peas and harvest the peas regularly to prolong the display and the crop.

### Stir-fried vegetable noodles

Heat 4 tablespoons vegetable oil and stir-fry a bunch of sliced spring onions and 2 thinly sliced carrots. Add 2 crushed garlic cloves, $1/4$ teaspoon dried chili flakes, 4 oz. (125 g) peas and 4 oz. (125 g) halved shiitake mushrooms and continue to stir-fry. Add 3 shredded Chinese cabbages and 8 oz. (250 g) cooked medium-sized egg noodles. Continue to stir-fry for 2 more minutes; stir in 2 tablespoons light soy sauce and 3 tablespoons hoisin sauce and serve.

# Cut-and-come-again

Cut-and-come-again crops are treated exactly as their name suggests: You cut the leaves for salads, usually when they are immature, allow them to regrow and then cut them again. Here we've used a mixture including radish 'Saisai', edible leaf carrot, cress 'Wrinkled Crinkles', kale 'Red Russian' and red amaranth. When sown directly they will germinate quickly and they will be ready to use within weeks.

## Ingredients

drainage material (see page 16)

all-purpose soil-less mix

1 square terra-cotta container, 20 x 8 in. (50 x 20 cm)

1 bamboo cane

1 packet of mixed salad greens seed

vermiculite or horticultural sand (optional)

## Method

1 Put plenty of drainage material in the base of a large, shallow container and fill to within 2 in. (5 cm) of the top with soil-less mix. Water the container thoroughly and allow the soil mix to drain.

2 Use a garden cane to mark straight, shallow rows, 3–4 in. (8–10 cm) apart on the surface of the soil.

3 Sow the seed thinly and cover lightly with sieved soil mix, vermiculite or horticultural sand. Water gently with a fine sprinkler attached to a watering can.

4 If necessary, thin out the germinating seedlings a little to prevent overcrowding and to allow weaker growing varieties to become established.

### Green and white pizza

Put 4 x 8 in. (20 cm) pita breads or sandwich wraps on baking sheets and scatter the centers with 7 oz. (200 g) crumbled Gorgonzola cheese. Bake in a preheated oven, 400°F (200°C) for 6–7 minutes or until the cheese has melted and the bread bases are crisp. Top the pizzas with slices of prosciutto and 2 oz. (50 g) salad greens. Add ground black pepper and drizzle some olive oil over the top.

# Super salad

Contrasting shapes, colors and textures make this group of salad crops as much a treat for the eye as for the taste buds. The filigree leaves of carrots form a soft centerpiece, while the handsome leaves and stems of 'Bull's Blood' beets are a colorful contrast. Bright green, frilly-leaved lettuce 'Fristina', which can be harvested a few leaves at a time, festoons the edge.

## Ingredients

1 packet of 'Bull's Blood' beet seed

1 packet of 'Yellowstone' carrot seed

1 packet of 'Fristina' lettuce seed

seed-starter mix

cell-pack trays

1 black, glazed square container,
    16 x 14 in. (40 x 35 cm)

drainage material (see page 16)

all-purpose soil-less mix

## Method

1  Sow the beet, carrot, and lettuce in seed-starter mix in cell-pack trays to get them started and sow a new batch every few weeks throughout the spring and summer to encourage repeat crops.

2  Put plenty of drainage material in the base of the container and fill with a good-quality, soil-less mix.

3  Transfer the seedlings as soon as they are large enough to handle. Space them fairly closely, planting a block of carrots in the center, surrounded by beets with the lettuce around the edges.

---

### Red cabbage and carrot slaw

Make the dressing by whisking together the juice of 1 orange, 1 tablespoon whole grain mustard, 1 crushed garlic clove and 3 tablespoons olive oil. Season to taste and let stand. Meanwhile, finely shred ¼ red cabbage and mix it with 1 sliced red onion, 1 grated carrot, 1 sliced orange and 2 oz. (50 g) dry roasted sliced almonds. Spoon the dressing over the mixture and serve.

# Tumbling toms

Tumbling tomatoes are well suited to growing in baskets and in an elevated position they will create an eyecatching show of glistening fruits that are convenient for picking. Both these cultivars bear a profusion of cherry-sized fruits. The fresh green, curled leaves of parsley are complemented by the glowing flowers of the annual climber *Thunbergia alata*.

## Ingredients

1 open-sided wire or wrought iron hanging basket, 14 in. (35 cm) across

1 synthetic-fiber hanging basket liner

all-purpose soil-less mix

water-retaining granules

1 parsley plant (*Petroselinum crispum*)

1 'Tumbling Tom Red' tomato plant

1 'Tumbling Tom Yellow' tomato plant

2 black-eyed Susan plants (*Thunbergia alata*) (non-edible)

## Method

**1** Choose a large open-sided wire or wrought iron hanging basket at least 14 in. (35 cm) in diameter and insert a liner. Follow the instructions for planting a hanging basket on page 17.

**2** Fill the hanging basket with a good-quality, soil-less mix with added water-retaining granules.

**3** Position the parsley in the center of the basket and a tomato on either side of it. Plant one black-eyed Susan plant in front of the parsley and one behind it. Leave the basket standing on a pot for a couple of weeks to settle before hanging in its final position.

**4** Water at least once a day and feed once a week with a liquid fertilizer to help sustain a worthwhile crop. Pinch out and train the shoots as necessary to maintain an attractive shape.

### Tomato and mozzarella bruschetta

Whisk together 3 tablespoons olive oil with 1 teaspoon balsamic vinegar, season to taste and stir in 12 halved bocconcini (baby mozzarella), 20 halved ripe cherry tomatoes and 2 tablespoons chopped basil. Barbecue or toast 4 slices of bread, rub each slice with ½ bruised garlic clove and drizzle over a little more oil. Arrange 4 oz. (125 g) arugula over the toast and spoon the tomato and mozzarella mixture on top. Garnish with basil leaves and serve.

# Towering thymes

A group of plastic drainage pipes of varying heights and diameters creates a funky home for a selection of plants. We've chosen a variety of thymes of differing habits and leaf colors from the gray-leaved woolly thyme to creamy white variegated 'Silver Posie'. As a textural contrast, one of the pipes hosts feathery-leaved carrots.

## Ingredients

6 plastic drainage pipes of varying heights and diameters

silver spray paint

bricks

6 plant pots of varying depths and diameters (to fit in the pipes)

all-purpose soil-less mix

horticultural sand

1 packet of 'Red Samurai' carrot seed

1 'Silver Posie' thyme plant (*Thymus vulgaris*)

1 lemon-variegated 'Golden King' thyme plant (*Thymus citriodorus*)

1 woolly thyme plant (*Thymus pseudolanuginosus*) (non-edible)

1 'Archer's Gold' thyme plant (*Thymus pulegioides*)

1 'Foxley' thyme plant (*Thymus pulegioides*)

horticultural grit

## Method

**1** Spray the drainage pipes with a suitable paint. Stand the bricks on end in the base of each pipe to prop up a plant pot so that the pots will sit inside without showing above the rims of the pipes.

**2** Fill a pot with a sandy soil mix (a mixture of soil-less mix and horticultural sand) to encourage long, straight roots. Sow a few carrot seeds in the top. Thin out the seedlings as necessary once they have germinated.

**3** Plant each thyme in a pot in all-purpose soil-less mix with added grit.

**4** Insert the pots into the pipes so that they stand on the bricks.

### Parsnip and thyme chips

Thinly slice 2 large parsnips and toss them in a bowl with 1 tablespoon all-purpose flour and 2 teaspoons thyme leaves to coat them. Deep-fry the parsnips in batches in vegetable oil for 2 minutes or until they are crisp and golden. Drain on paper towels.

# Lettuce and tulips

Add an extra dimension to your pots by combining spring-flowering bulbs with colorful early salad leaf crops. The red flowers and mottled foliage of the tulips are set off to perfection by the purple violets and 'Lollo Rossa' lettuce.

## Ingredients

9 dwarf tulip bulbs, such as *Tulipa* 'Red Riding Hood' (non-edible)

1 plastic pot, 7¼ in. (18.5 cm) in diameter

all-purpose soil-less mix

1 packet of 'Lollo Rossa' lettuce seed

cell-pack trays

seed-starter mix

8 purple violet plants

1 hexagonal terra-cotta container, 16 x 12 in. (40 x 30 cm)

drainage material (see page 16)

## Method

1 In autumn plant the tulips in a plastic pot, 7¼ in. (18.5 cm) in diameter, filled with soil-less mix to start them into growth, ready to transfer to a more decorative pot in the spring.

2 In early spring sow the lettuce in seed-starter mix in cell-pack trays and put them in a cold frame to germinate. As soon as the lettuce plants are ready for planting, buy eight young violet plants.

3 Put plenty of drainage material in the base of the hexagonal terra-cotta pot and fill with a good-quality, soil-less mix. Transfer the tulips to the center of the pot and plant the violets evenly spaced in a ring around the tulips. Then encircle the violets in turn with seedling lettuce.

4 Deadhead the violets to keep them blooming for as long as possible and pick the lettuce leaves a few at a time, as required.

---

### Red leaf salad with pecan cheese balls

Arrange 6 oz. (175 g) lettuce leaves and a handful of edible flowers in a bowl. Add ½ sliced red onion and spoon a yogurt or sweet mustard dressing on top. Make the cheese balls by mixing together 8 oz. (250 g) goat cheese or cream cheese with 1½ oz. (40 g) finely chopped pecans. Shape the mixture into 16 balls and lightly roll them in paprika. Chill for 20 minutes before serving.

# Stir-fry

An inexpensive plastic pot is turned into an appropriate home for this selection of leafy Chinese vegetables by wrapping it with a roll of bamboo border edging. The plants here are grown for their tender young leaves and can be used in salads or stir-fries.

## Ingredients

1 packet of bok choy seed, such as 'Mei Qing'

1 packet of mizuna greens seed

1 packet of spinach mustard seed

1 packet of red-leaved mustard seed, such as 'Red Giant'

cell-pack trays

seed-starter mix

1 square plastic, terra-cotta or wooden container, 20 x 8 in. (50 x 20 cm)

1 roll of bamboo border edging, 6 ft. 6 in. (2 m) long and 10 in. (25 cm) high

plastic-coated wire

drainage material (see page 16)

all-purpose soil-less mix

## Method

1 Sow the seeds in seed-starter mix in cell-pack trays, allowing plenty of spares, or sow direct into the container and thin out as necessary. Make successive sowings every few weeks to have a continuous supply of leaves.

2 Use a plain, shallow, square pot and wrap a length of bamboo border edging, available from garden centers, around it. Fasten the ends together with plastic-coated wire. Put plenty of drainage material in the base and fill with soil-less mix.

3 When they are large enough to handle, plant the seedlings in rows to create a striped effect. Repeat each variety a couple of times to create a more even and interesting spread of leaf color. Water well during dry spells.

### Sesame shrimp with bok choy

Mix together 1 teaspoon sesame oil, 2 tablespoons light soy sauce, 1 tablespoon honey, 1 teaspoon grated fresh ginger root, 1 teaspoon crushed garlic and 1 tablespoon lemon juice and use the mixture to marinate 1 lb. 3 oz. (600 g) raw peeled tiger shrimp (tails left on) for 5–10 minutes. Cut 1 lb. (500 g) bok choy in half, blanch for 40–50 seconds and drain. Heat 2 tablespoons vegetable oil and cook the shrimp in the marinade for 3–4 minutes. Arrange the bak choy on plates with the shrimp and pan juices on top.

# Sunny show

Brightly colored dwarf sunflowers jostle with low-growing, red- and white-flowered runner beans in this lively planting. There are many varieties of dwarf sunflowers that grow to heights between 18–24 in. (45–60 cm), including 'Dwarf Yellow Spray' that has many relatively small heads on each plant. In front is runner bean 'Hestia' that will grow to the same height as the sunflowers but has a more relaxed habit.

## Ingredients

1 packet of dwarf runner bean 'Hestia' seed

3 dwarf sunflower plants, such as 'Dwarf Yellow Spray', or a packet of seed

biodegradable peat pots

seed-starter mix

1 fiberglass trough that looks like it is made of lead, 24 x 8 in. (60 x 20 cm)

drainage material (see page 16)

all-purpose soil-less mix

well-rotted garden compost or manure

6 thin sticks, 12–18 in. (30–45 cm) long, to support runner beans

soluble fertilizer

## Method

**1** Sow the beans and sunflowers into seed-starter mix in individual biodegradable peat pots that will slowly disintegrate and avoid root disturbance.

**2** Make sure there are drainage holes in the trough. Put plenty of drainage material in the base of the trough and fill it with a good-quality, soil-less mix with added organic matter, such as well-rotted garden compost or manure, for moisture retention.

**3** When they are large enough, plant the sunflowers, spacing them evenly along the back of the trough, with five or six runner beans along the front edge. Push sticks into the soil to provide support for the beans and sunflowers. Water well and feed occasionally with a soluble fertilizer.

### Stir-fried hoisin beans

Blanch 1 lb. (500 g) beans in boiling water for 2 minutes, then drain well. Heat 2 tablespoons of vegetable oil in a wok, add 2 sliced garlic cloves and 2 red chilies that have been deseeded and sliced. Stir briefly, then add the beans, 6 tablespoons of hoisin sauce, and 1 teaspoon of salt to the wok. Stir-fry over a high heat for 1–2 minutes until the beans are tender. Serve immediately with plain boiled rice or noodles.

# Lettuce and lobelia

Few leafy vegetables are as versatile, easy-to-grow, and as visually appealing as lettuce. It can be grown in baskets, window boxes and many other types of containers and either allowed to mature and be harvested whole or, in the case of many varieties, treated as a cut-and-come-again crop. Interplanting the lettuce with non-edible, pale blue-flowered trailing annual lobelia makes for a striking contrast.

## Ingredients

1 packet of mixed colored-leafed lettuce seed

seed-starter mix

cell-pack trays

15 pale blue trailing lobelia plants (non-edible)

1 wrought iron or plastic-coated metal half-hanging basket, 16 in. (40 cm) across

hanging basket liner

all-purpose soil-less mix

## Method

1 Sow the lettuce in tiny pinches in seed-starter mix in cell-pack trays in mid- to late spring and place them in a cold frame or sheltered place where they will germinate readily. Overcrowded bunches of seedlings should be thinned down to one strong plant.

2 Buy the lobelia plants from a nursery or garden center once the lettuces are large enough to plant. Choose a large, hayrack-style half-basket, 16 in. (40 cm) across, and insert a liner. Using soil-less mix, follow the instructions for planting a hanging basket on page 17.

3 Make sure that the plants are evenly distributed over the sides and top of the basket and water well. Attach the basket to a wall or fence in a sunny but not scorchingly hot position. Keep well watered to prevent the lettuce from bolting.

### Thai-dressed rolls

Put 8 lettuce leaves in boiling water for 10 seconds. Rinse and drain them. Shred 16 more lettuce leaves and mix with 9 oz. (275 g) diced tofu and 3½ oz. (100 g) shredded snow peas. Mix together 2 tablespoons sesame oil, 2 tablespoons soy sauce, 2 tablespoons lime juice, 1 tablespoon light brown sugar, 1 sliced Thai chili, and 1 crushed garlic clove. Mix the sauce and tofu mixture and spoon into the lettuce leaves. Roll up and chill.

# Summer cocktail

What could be better on a warm summer evening than to be able to pick fresh flowers, fruits or leaves to add a refreshing taste to a summer beverage? Tiny alpine strawberries, borage, and salad burnet are among the best greens for this purpose, and a galvanized steel bucket is an unusual but somehow fitting home for them.

## Ingredients

1 galvanized metal bucket,
   12 in. (30 cm) across

drainage material (see page 16)

all-purpose soil-less mix

slow-release fertilizer

water-retaining granules

1 borage plant (*Borago officinalis*)

3 salad burnet plants (*Sanguisorba minor*)

4 alpine strawberry plants

## Method

**1** Drill several large drainage holes in the bottom of the bucket. Wear goggles to protect your eyes from metal splinters. Drop in a layer of drainage material.

**2** Fill the bucket with good-quality, soil-less mix with a few added slow-release fertilizer granules and water-retaining granules.

**3** Plant the borage in the center of the container, the salad burnet around it, and the strawberries around the edge so the fruit will drape over the rim.

---

### Strawberry lemonade

Put 4 fl. oz. (100 ml) sugar syrup, 10 strawberries and 10 mint leaves in a blender or food processor and blend to a purée. Transfer the purée to a large pitcher, add 4 fl. oz. (100 ml) fresh lemon juice, 1¾ pints (1 liter) soda water and plenty of ice cubes and stir well. Serve in goblets decorated with strawberry slices, sprigs of mint, and borage flowers.

# Fish lovers bouquet

Handy for the kitchen, this selection of herbs will provide a summer-long supply of fresh leaves that can be used in a variety of recipes, especially fish dishes. French tarragon is a versatile herb with a strong, distinctive flavor that complements chicken, veal, and rice dishes, as well as fish.

## Ingredients

1 wooden window box, 24 x 8 in. (60 x 20 cm)

drainage material (see page 16)

all-purpose soil-less mix

horticultural grit

1 French tarragon (*Artemisia dracunculus*)

2 dill plants (*Anethum graveolens*); choose a dwarf variety, such as 'Bouquet'

2 parsley plants (*Petroselinum crispum*)

3 lemon-variegated thyme 'Golden King' plants (*Thymus citriodorus*)

2 'Silver Posie' thyme plants (*Thymus vulgaris*)

## Method

1 Make sure there are adequate drainage holes in the base of the window box. Add a layer of drainage material and fill with good-quality, soil-less mix with added grit so that it will drain freely.

2 Plant the tarragon at the back in the center with the dill on either side and the parsley at each end. Alternate the thymes in a row in front where they will gently tumble over the edge of the trough.

3 Harvest the leaves a few at a time, when you need them. After flowering, trim back the thyme to keep it bushy and encourage a fresh new crop of leaves. Take care not to overwater this container because the tarragon, especially, will resent being too wet.

### Chicken and tarragon salad

Put a 3 lb. (1.5 kg) chicken in a saucepan with 1 sliced onion, the juice and rind of 1 orange, 1 tablespoon chopped tarragon, and 1 bay leaf. Cover with water and simmer for 45–60 minutes. When the chicken is cooked and cool, cut it into pieces. Mix ½ pint (300 ml) of the cooled-down stock with 1 tablespoon olive oil and 1 tablespoon white wine vinegar and pour over the chicken. Garnish with oranges, watercress, and sprigs of tarragon.

# Ornamental onions

Spring onions are partnered with spinach in this old wooden crate to provide several weeks' worth of tasty salad ingredients, utilizing every square inch of space. Spinach is a highly nutritious crop packed with iron and vitamins. The leaves can either be lightly steamed or the fresh young ones in particular can be eaten in salads.

## Ingredients

1 packet of onion 'Red Beard' (or similar) seed

1 packet of onion 'Shimonita' (or similar) seed

cell-pack trays

seed-starter mix

1 wooden crate, 18 x 12 in. (45 x 30 cm)

plastic sheets

drainage material (see page 16)

all-purpose soil-less mix

1 packet of spinach 'Bordeaux' seed

## Method

**1** Sow the onions in seed-starter mix in cell-pack trays, one or two seeds per compartment and place in a cold frame to germinate.

**2** Line the wooden crate with the plastic sheets and pierce plenty of holes in the base for drainage. Add a layer of drainage material and fill with good-quality, soil-less mix. Once they are large enough to handle, plant the onions in rows. Initially they can be quite closely spaced, then gradually thinned out, with the harvested leaves being put to good use in salads.

**3** Let the remaining onions mature for use later, and sow spinach directly into the soil between them. Cover lightly with soil mix. The spinach will germinate rapidly and should be harvested as baby leaves to avoid affecting the development of the onions.

### Pear, Stilton, and spinach salad

Core and thickly slice 4 pears and cook the slices for 1 minute on each side on a hot griddle. Sprinkle them with 4 tablespoons lemon juice. Pile 8 oz. (250 g) baby spinach on a large plate and arrange the pear slices on top. Sprinkle 4 chopped walnuts and 8 oz. (250 g) crumbled Stilton cheese on top. Spoon 4 tablespoons walnut oil over the salad and serve.

# Main courses

Red and gold **58**

Potted potager **60**

Pods and cobs **62**

Perfect partners **64**

Floral feast **66**

Select salad **68**

Sky high **70**

Winter vegetable cubes **72**

Pasta and pizza pot **74**

Once upon a time **76**

Textural treats **78**

Mint medley **80**

On fire! **82**

Potato paradise **84**

Peas and beans **86**

Pretty in purple **88**

Roots and shoots **90**

Red devil **92**

Pepper pot **94**

Purple and bronze **96**

A taste of the Mediterranean **98**

Kale and cabbage **100**

On the bay **102**

Fireball **104**

Green garnish **106**

Lots of leaves **108**

# Red and gold

The small, round, golden-yellow zucchini 'One Ball' is a compact, prolific variety that provides solid contrast with the orange-red-fruited bush tomato 'Czech's Bush'. These are both thirsty, greedy plants, so water and feed regularly for a good, sustained crop.

## Ingredients

2 zucchini 'One Ball' plants or a packet of seeds

small plastic plant pots

seed-starter mix

1 glazed cylindrical container, 18 x 16 in. (45 x 40 cm), neutral brown or green

1 self-watering container kit, 16 in. (40 cm) across (see page 24)

all-purpose soil-less mix

1 'Czech's Bush' tomato plant or similar bush variety

3–4 bamboo canes, 4 ft. (1.2 m)  long

## Method

**1** If you are starting from seed, sow the zucchini in seed-starter mix in small individual pots in mid- to late spring and place in a heated propagator. Alternatively, sow them in an unheated greenhouse once all danger of frost has passed.

**2** Set up the self-watering container kit inside the glazed container, fill with good-quality, soil-less mix and plant the tomato and zucchini plants in a triangle. Water well and feed regularly. The tomato may need a bamboo cane or two to support its weight when it is laden with fruit. Pinch out the tip of the tomato plant to encourage it to bush out.

**3** Regularly remove some of the oldest zucchini leaves to allow air and sunlight through to ripen the fruit and also prevent the tomato from being swamped. Pick the zucchini when they are just 3 in. (7.5 cm) across to produce fruits all season long.

### Linguine with summer vegetables

Slice 1 red pepper, 1 zucchini, 1 red onion, and 1 small eggplant. Trim  8 asparagus spears and cook all the vegetables in a hot frying pan. Transfer to a dish and add 3 tablespoons cooked peas. Drizzle with 5 tablespoons olive oil and keep warm while you cook 10 oz. (300 g) linguine. Mix the cooked pasta and vegetables together, season to taste and scatter grated Parmesan cheese on top. Garnish with torn basil leaves and serve.

# Potted potager

A mouth-watering mixture of vegetables, edible flowers, and herbs will provide produce all summer long. Housing them in a deep, generous-sized container makes it easy to grow a wide range of produce in a small space.

## Ingredients

1 packet of compact-growing kale seed (such as 'Dwarf Green Curled')

1 packet of nasturtium seed (*Tropaeolum majus*)

1 packet of 'Bull's Blood' beet seed

seed-starter mix

cell-pack trays

1 square wooden container, 30 x 18 in. (75 x 45 cm)

plastic sheets

drainage material (see page 16)

all-purpose soil-less mix

soil-based potting mix

1 'Silver Posie' thyme plant (*Thymus vulgaris*)

1 parsley plant (*Petroselinum crispum*)

2 perpetual-fruiting strawberry plants

1 coriander plant (*Coriandrum sativum*)

1 dill plant (*Anethum graveolens*)

1 garlic or Chinese chives plant (*Allium tuberosum*)

6 purple and white violet plants

## Method

**1** In spring, sow the various seeds in seed-starter mix in cell-pack trays and put them in a cold frame to germinate. You will need only a few plants of each variety, so don't oversow.

**2** Position the wooden container before lining it and filling it with soil mix and plants, because it will be too heavy to move afterwards. Line the sides of the container with the plastic sheets to prolong its life (but do not cover the drainage holes). Place a layer of drainage material in the base and fill with a half-and-half mix of soil-less and soil-based mixes.

**3** Once the seedlings are ready for planting out, purchase the other plants. Position the bought plants first and plant the seedlings in small informal blocks between them. Taller varieties, such as coriander, should be planted toward the center of the container and trailing or low-growing plants, such as strawberries and thyme, should be planted toward the edge.

---

### Falafel cakes

Blend 13 oz. (400 g) canned chickpeas with 1 onion, 3 garlic cloves, 2 teaspoons cumin seeds, 1 teaspoon mild chili powder, 2 tablespoons chopped garlic chives, 2 tablespoons chopped mint, 3 tablespoons chopped coriander and 2 oz. (50 g) bread crumbs. Season to taste. Flatten spoonfuls of the mixture into cakes and fry in batches in ½ in. (1 cm) vegetable oil for about 3 minutes, turning once, until golden.

# Pods and cobs

A half-barrel is needed for tall, thirsty, fast-growing crops such as sweet corn. 'Minipop' has been bred to be harvested as a mini vegetable, producing succulent "baby" cobs. An underplanting of dwarf French beans covers and shades the soil at the base of the corn.

## Ingredients

1 packet of sweet corn 'Minipop' seed

1 packet of dwarf French green bean 'Purple Teepee' seed

1 packet of dwarf French green bean 'Golden Teepee' seed

plastic pots, 3 in. (7.5 cm) in diameter

seed-starter mix

1 wooden half-barrel, 28 x 16 in. (70 x 40 cm)

drainage material (see page 16)

all-purpose soil-less mix

well-rotted garden compost or manure

## Method

1 Sow the beans in seed-starter mix in individual pots in mid-spring and put them in a heated propagator or greenhouse to germinate. Alternatively, sow them later in spring in a frost-free greenhouse or cold frame.

2 Drill plenty of drainage holes in the base of the barrel, cover them with a layer of drainage material and fill with a good-quality, soil-less mix. Mix in additional organic matter, such as well-rotted garden compost or manure to improve moisture retention. Position the container where it will receive as much sun as possible.

3 Sow the sweet corn seed directly in the barrel. Thin out the seedlings until you have just five or six evenly spaced sweet corn plants around the container. When the beans are big enough, plant six of each type of bean between them. Harvest the beans regularly to keep them producing and pick the corn as mini cobs before the grains begin to swell. Keep well watered and feed regularly.

---

### Grilled sweet corn with chili and lime

Remove the husks from 4 corn cobs. Mix together 1 tablespoon coarse chili powder and 1 tablespoon sea salt. Cook the sweet corn under a broiler for 4–5 minutes, turning them regularly so they cook all over and are slightly charred in places. Dip half a lime in the chili mixture and squeeze it over the corn. Repeat with 3 more halves of lime to coat the corn cobs and serve immediately.

# Perfect partners

These containers combine edible plants with some that are purely ornamental to produce flowers and crops all summer long. Each of the three tall, circular containers is sown with a single crop that can be harvested as mini-vegetables or young leaves and replaced halfway through the season or left to mature. Each crop is surrounded by tender perennial trailing plants to create a set of stunning pairings.

## Ingredients

1 packet of lettuce 'Revolution' seed

1 packet of leek 'Armor' seed

1 packet of beet 'Kestrel' seed

cell-pack trays

seed-starter mix

1 round zinc, silver-colored container,
  14 x 12 in. (35 x 30 cm)

1 round zinc, silver-colored container,
  16 x 14 in. (40 x 35 cm)

1 round zinc, silver-colored container,
  20 x 16 in. (50 x 40 cm)

drainage material (see page 16)

all-purpose soil-less mix

4 strawflower 'Frosted Sulphur' plants
  (non-edible)

5 Verbena 'Aztec Magic Plum' plants
  (non-edible)

4 Portulaca 'Sundial Mango' plants
  (non-edible)

## Method

1  Sow the vegetables in seed-starter mix in cell-pack trays in mid- to late spring. You will need only a few for each container, so don't sow too many unless you need them elsewhere.

2  If necessary, drill holes in the base of each container and add a layer of drainage material before filling with soil-less mix.

3  Plant three lettuce surrounded by strawflowers in the largest container, and three or four leeks skirted by verbena in the medium-sized pot. In the smallest container plant a central block of five beets, with the portulaca planted around the edge. Have a few later-sown plants on hand to replace crops as they are harvested, because the tender perennials will continue until frosts arrive.

### Arugula, beet, and red pepper salad

Cut 4 cooked beets into 6–8 pieces, drizzle with olive oil and roast in a preheated oven, 400°F (200°C), for 30 minutes. Blend 1 oz. (25 g) roasted hazelnuts with 1 tablespoon balsamic vinegar, 1 garlic clove, and 4 tablespoons olive or hazelnut oil. Arrange 3 oz. (75 g) arugula leaves, 10 oz. (300 g) charbroiled red peppers and the beets on a plate. Drizzle the dressing over them.

# Floral feast

A surprising number of flowers are edible. This summery feast of edible flowers includes pot marigolds, violets, nasturtiums, cornflowers, and sunflowers.

## Ingredients

1 packet of sunflower 'Teddy Bear' seed (*Helianthus annuus*)

1 packet of pot marigold 'Pink Surprise' seed (*Calendula officinalis*)

1 packet of dwarf cornflower 'Florence blue' seed (*Centaurea cyanus*)

1 packet of nasturtium 'Moonlight' seed (*Tropaeolum majus*)

1 packet of nasturtium 'Empress of India' seed (*Tropaeolum majus* )

cell-pack trays

seed-starter mix

selection of terra-cotta plant pots of varying shapes and sizes, including
   1 tall pot 14 x 18 in. (35 x 45 cm),
   1 trough 20 x 8 in. (50 x 20 cm),
   2 pots 14 x 10 in. (35 x 25 cm) and
   1 small pot 4 x 4 in. (10 x 10 cm)

drainage material (see page 16)

all-purpose soil-less mix

6 purple and white viola plants

6 yellow viola plants

1 lavender 'Princess Blue' plant (*Lavandula angustifolila*)

6 pale blue and cream violet plants

## Method

1  Sow the various seeds in seed-starter mix in cell-pack trays in mid-spring and put them in a cold frame. When the seedlings are large enough for transplanting, buy the lavender and violet plants ready for planting.

2  Put plenty of drainage material in the bases of the terra-cotta pots and fill them with soil-less mix. Plant three sunflowers in a tall pot surrounded by purple and white violets, six pot marigolds surrounded by a ring of seven or eight cornflowers in a bowl, the nasturtiums and yellow violets in a trough, the lavender as a single specimen plant, and the three pale blue and cream violets in a small pot.

3  If possible, have a couple of spare pots of later-sown plants waiting in the wings to replace any of the original plantings once they are past their prime. Deadhead regularly so the plants do not divert their energies into seed rather than flower production.

---

### Cottage garden salad

Put about 8 oz. (250 g) torn mixed salad leaves, such as arugula, escarole, red oakleaf, salad burnet, curly chicory, radicchio, and lamb's lettuce, into a salad bowl with a handful of nasturtiums and fresh herb sprigs with their flowers, such as fennel, chives, dill and mint. Hull and halve 8 oz. (250 g) small strawberries and add them to the salad bowl. Season to taste, spoon over a yogurt or orange dressing and serve.

# Select salad

Striking edible leaves and stunning blooms combine to create this colorful collection of unusual salad ingredients. The rich green, highly nutritional leaves of parsley are invaluable not only for garnishing but also for enhancing the flavor of foods as well.

## Ingredients

1 packet of pot marigold 'Greenheart Orange' seed (*Calendula officinalis*)

1 packet of blood-veined sorrel seed (*Rumex acetosa*)

1 packet of variegated American or land cress seed (*Barbarea vulgaris* 'Variegata')

cell-pack trays

seed-starter mix

1 fiberglass container that looks like it is made of lead, 12 x 12 in. (30 x 30 cm)

drainage material (see page 16)

all-purpose soil-less mix

2 parsley plants (*Petroselinum crispum*)

## Method

**1** Sow the various seeds in seed-starter mix in cell-pack trays in a cold frame in the spring and move to a sheltered spot outdoors once the plants have germinated and are growing strongly.

**2** When the seedlings are large enough, transfer them to a container, adding a layer of drainage material to the container before filling with soil-less mix. Buy two young parsley plants to accompany them. Plant one pot marigold in the center and surround with a ring of alternating parsley, sorrel, and land cress plants, using two plants of each.

**3** Pick leaves regularly, whether you intend to use them or not, because this will encourage fresh, tasty new growth. Remove faded pot marigold blooms to prevent them from running to seed.

---

### Herb omelette

Mix 1 tablespoon whole grain mustard with 1½ oz (40 g) unsalted butter and spread the mixture over the undersides of 4 flat mushrooms. Broil for 5–6 minutes. Meanwhile, beat 2 tablespoons chopped mixed herbs (such as chives, parsley, and tarragon) with 4 eggs and season to taste. Melt about ½ oz. (15 g) butter in a nonstick frying pan, swirl in the egg mixture and cook. Slide the omelette onto a warmed plate, add the mushrooms and serve.

# Sky high

Planted in a capacious wooden half-barrel and clambering up a wigwam, golden-leaved, scarlet-flowered runner bean 'Sun Bright' is as ornamental a climber as you could wish for. For an extra splash of color we've added blue-flowered morning glories to create a truly breathtaking combination.

## Ingredients

1 packet of runner bean 'Sun Bright' seed

seed-starter mix

plastic pots, 3 in. (7.5 cm) in diameter

1 packet of morning glory 'Heavenly Blue' seed (*Ipomoea*) or a similar cultivar (non-edible)

cell-pack trays

1 wooden half-barrel, 28 x 16 in. (70 x 40 cm)

drainage material (see page 16)

all-purpose soil-less mix

1 willow obelisk, 5 ft. (1.5 m) high, or 6 bamboo canes, each 6 ft. (1.8 m) long

## Method

**1** Sow the runner beans in seed-starter mix in individual pots and the morning glories in cell-pack trays in spring. Place in a heated propagating case or heated greenhouse to germinate. When they are large enough, transfer the morning glories into large pots.

**2** Drill plenty of drainage holes in the base of the barrel and cover with a layer of drainage material. Fill with good-quality, soil-less mix. Transfer the beans and the morning glories to a large container once all danger of frost has passed. A half-barrel should accommodate five of each, planted alternately.

**3** Provide support in the form of a willow obelisk or a wigwam of bamboo canes, at least 5 ft. (1.5 m) high, and wind in the shoots to stop them becoming too tangled. Feed and water regularly.

### Green vegetable risotto

Heat 2 oz. (50 g) butter and 1 tablespoon olive oil and sauté a crushed garlic clove and a chopped onion. Add 10 oz. (300 g) arborio rice and stir, then gradually add 1¾ pints (1 liter) hot vegetable stock and stir constantly, until it has been absorbed. Add 4 oz. (125 g) each of trimmed runner beans, peas, broad beans, asparagus, and spinach, and stir in 3 fl. oz. (75 ml) dry vermouth or white wine. Cook, stirring, for another 2 minutes, then stir in 2 oz. (50 g) butter, 2 tablespoons chopped parsley, and grated Parmesan cheese.

# Winter vegetable cubes

These handsome containers play host to a trio of good-looking vegetables planted in blocks to create a stunning autumn and winter display. Once harvested, the cauliflower planter can be moved away, leaving the chard and kale to continue looking stunning throughout the winter. The mulch not only looks great but will also help conserve moisture.

## Ingredients

1 packet of cauliflower 'Candid Charm' seed

1 packet of kale 'Redbor' seed

1 packet of red-stemmed chard or Swiss chard seed

cell-pack trays

seed-starter mix

1 square, charcoal-gray, terrazzo, reconstituted-stone container, 16 x 16 in. (40 x 40 cm)

1 square, charcoal-gray, terrazzo, reconstituted-stone container, 14 x 14 in. (35 x 35 cm)

1 charcoal-gray, terrazzo, reconstituted-stone trough, 20 x 12 in. (50 x 30 cm)

drainage material (see page 16)

all-purpose soil-less mix

slate chips or polished pebbles

## Method

**1** Sow the seeds in late spring or early summer in seed-starter mix in cell-pack trays for an autumn or early-winter crop. The kale can be harvested as baby leaves, so make subsequent sowing through the first half of summer, allowing the final batch of seedlings to mature fully.

**2** When the seedlings are large enough, plant the kale in the largest container in a block of nine, the chard or leaf beet in the smaller square container, again in a block of nine, and the cauliflower in a row of three in the planter. Using soil-less mix, follow the instructions for planting a container on page 16.

**3** Mulch around each group of plants with slate or pebbles and keep well watered. Be on the lookout for caterpillars and pick them off immediately.

### Cauliflower tarka

Cook 1 teaspoon cumin seeds and 1 teaspoon yellow mustard seeds in 1 tablespoon sunflower oil. Add 1 lb. (500 g) cauliflower florets, 2 finely chopped garlic cloves, 1 in. (2.5 cm) fresh ginger root, shredded, 2 sliced red chilies and stir-fry for 6–7 minutes. Stir in ½ teaspoon garam masala and 7 fl. oz. (200 ml) hot water. Cover and cook on high for 1–2 minutes. Season to taste and serve.

# Pasta and pizza pot

A dwarf bush tomato plant, which will yield a hefty crop of tasty fruits, can be surrounded by a mixture of marjorams with various leaf colors, including gold-tipped, golden curly, and variegated forms, and oregano to add color and texture. Annual arugula, which has finely cut leaves and attractive spikes of pale yellow flowers, completes the planting.

## Ingredients

1 fiberglass container that looks like it is made of lead, 16 x 16 in. (40 x 40 cm)

drainage material (see page 16)

all-purpose soil-less mix

1 tomato 'Totem' plant

1–2 bamboo canes, about 4 ft. (1.2 m) long

1 oregano or wild marjoram plant (*Origanum vulgare*)

1 golden curly marjoram plant (*Origanum vulgare* 'Aureum Crispum')

1 golden marjoram plant (*Origanum vulgare* 'Aureum')

1 variegated marjoram plant (*Origanum vulgare* 'Country Cream')

1 'Gold Tip' marjoram plant (*Origanum vulgare*)

1 packet of cut-leaved annual arugula seed (*Eruca vesicaria*)

## Method

**1** Make sure there are plenty of drainage holes in the base of the container. Cover them with a layer of drainage material and fill with soil-less mix.

**2** Plant the tomato in the center of the pot and push in a couple of bamboo canes for support. Evenly space the various marjorams around the tomato near the edge of the pot so they will tumble forward and obscure the straight lines of the container.

**3** Sprinkle the arugula seeds thinly over the surface of the soil mix in the gaps between the other plants and cover with a light dusting of sieved soil mix. Water well. Because it is fast maturing, the arugula will have just enough time to get established before the other plants fill out.

### Pizza napoletana

Make or buy 2 x 9 in. (23 cm) pizza bases. Brush them with olive oil, then divide among them 13 oz. (400 g) canned chopped and drained tomatoes, 1 tablespoon chopped basil, 2 teaspoons fresh oregano, 6 oz. (175 g) sliced mozzarella cheese, and 4 tablespoons grated Parmesan cheese. Bake in a preheated oven, at 425°F (220°C), for 15 minutes, then reduce the heat to 350°F (180°C) for 5 minutes.

# Once upon a time

Eggplants are one of the most attractive of all fruiting vegetables. As well as the glossy, deep purple, pink-purple, pale green, or white fruits, they bear pretty mauve flowers and handsome feltlike leaves. They grow well in containers, where it is easy to control watering but make sure they never get too dry or too wet.

## Ingredients

1 'Fairytale' eggplant plant or
  a packet of seed

cell-pack trays

seed-starter mix

1 packet of dwarf runner bean
  'Snow White' seed

biodegradable peat pots

plastic pots, 3 in. (7.5 cm) in diameter

1 light gray, terrazzo, reconstituted-
  stone container,
  20 x 18 in. (50 x 45 cm)

drainage material (see page 16)

all-purpose soil-less mix

well-rotted manure or garden compost

## Method

1 Sow the eggplants in seed-starter mix in cell-packs trays in a heated greenhouse or propagating case. Sow the runner beans in individual peat pots two or three weeks later because they mature more quickly than the eggplants. When they large enough to handle, transplant the eggplants into small plastic pots.

2 Transfer outdoors when all danger of frost has passed. Add a layer of drainage material to the container before filling with a good-quality, soil-less mix, adding extra organic matter such as well-rotted manure. Position the eggplant in the center, surrounded by a ring of beans spaced about 4 in. (10 cm) apart.

3 Feed and water regularly. Gently mist over the runner bean flowers occasionally to help them set, and pick the beans when they are young and tender.

### Tomato and eggplant parmigiana

Slice a large eggplant and fry in olive oil until golden brown. Cut 1 lb. (500 g) ripe red plum tomatoes into wedges and arrange them in alternate layers with the eggplant in a shallow ovenproof dish, sprinkling a total of 2 oz. (50 g) grated Parmesan cheese between the layers. Season to taste and bake them in a preheated oven, 375°F (190°C), for 15–20 minutes. Garnish with parsley and serve immediately or at room temperature.

# Textural treats

This collection of delicate edible flowers and tasty leaves is complemented by wispy grasses to create a hazy summer display that looks, tastes, and smells great. Both the blue-flowered hyssop and pinkish lavender Mexican hyssop attract bees, so this is the perfect container to site among your pots of beans, tomatoes, and other fruiting plants to ensure their blooms are well pollinated and plenty of fruit sets.

## Ingredients

1 wooden crate, 24 x 12 in. (60 x 30 cm)

plastic sheet

drainage material (see page 16)

all-purpose soil-less mix

2 Mexican hyssop 'Lavender Haze' plants (*Agastache pallidiflora* x *neomexicana*) (non-edible)

3 hyssop plants (*Hyssopus officinalis*)

5 small Esparto grass plants (*Stipa tenuissima*) (non-edible)

2 New Zealand sedge 'Frosted Curls' plants (*Carex comans*) (non-edible)

3 coriander plants (*Coriandrum sativum*)

2 common thyme plants (*Thymus vulgaris*)

2 mother of thyme plants (*Thymus coccineus* Group)

1 packet of summer savory seed (*Satureja hortensis*)

## Method

**1** Line the crate with the plastic sheet and pierce holes in the bottom. Cover the drainage holes with a layer of drainage material and fill to within 4 in. (10 cm) of the top with soil-less mix.

**2** While they are still in their pots, lay all the plants out on the surface of the soil mix in a random fashion to be sure that you are happy with their position before planting. Once planted, fill in with more soil mix, firm gently, and water thoroughly. Sow summer savory seeds in between to fill in the gaps.

**3** Remove faded flowering stems from both the hyssops to encourage new flowering shoots to form and lightly trim the thymes after flowering.

### Fried snapper with red onions and thyme

Cook 2 sliced red onions in a hot frying pan until soft. Add a handful of chopped thyme and push to the side of the pan. Cook 4 snapper fillets, each about 6 oz. (175 g), for about 4 minutes on each side. Serve with the onions and thyme and drizzle with olive oil.

# Mint medley

Because they are notoriously invasive, mints are best grown in separate pots where their wayward habits can be kept in check. Tall, slender terra-cotta pots and chimney pots of varying heights show each mint off to perfection.

## Ingredients

1 packet of chard or leaf beet 'Bright Lights' seed

cell-pack trays

seed-starter mix

plastic pots, 3 in. (7.5 cm) in diameter

2 deep plastic plant pots

drainage material (see page 16)

all-purpose soil-less mix

1 pennyroyal plant (*Mentha pulegium*)

1 Moroccan mint plant (*Mentha spicata* var. *crispa* 'Moroccan')

1 eau-de-cologne mint plant (*Mentha* x *piperita* f. *citrata*)

1 pineapple mint plant (*Mentha suaveolens* 'Variegata')

1 Corsican mint plant (*Mentha requienii*)

2 recycled chimney pots or similar

1 ribbed terra-cotta pot, 14 x 24 in. (35 x 60 cm)

1 ribbed terra-cotta pot, 10 x 16 in. (25 x 40 cm)

1 plain terra-cotta pot, 9 x 12 in. (23 x 30 cm)

## Method

1 Sow the chard or leaf beet in seed-starter mix in cell-pack trays and transplant into small individual pots when the seedlings are large enough to handle.

2 Choose two plastic pots—preferably deep ones in which climbing plants are sold —to sit inside the chimney pots.

3 Following the instructions for planting a container on page 16, pot up each of the mints individually using soil-less mix. Pot the pennyroyal and the Moroccan mint into the plastic pots and plant the eau-de-cologne and pineapple mints directly into the tallest and shortest pots. Plant a single chard in the center of the medium-sized pot. Split the Corsican mint into four or five pieces and plant them around the base of the chard.

4 Place the plastic pots inside the chimney pots. When the plants become pot-bound, lift and split the mints, then replant a smaller portion. Pick leaves regularly for garnishing.

### Minted rice with tomato and bean sprouts

Finely chop 6 spring onions and 2 garlic cloves and stir-fry them for 2–3 minutes in 2 tablespoons olive oil. Add 1½ lb. (750 g) cooked, cooled Basmati rice and cook for an additional 3–4 minutes. Stir in 2 finely chopped ripe plum tomatoes and 8 oz. (250 g) mixed bean sprouts (such as aduki, mung, lentil, and chickpea sprouts) and cook for 2–3 minutes. Stir in a small handful of mint leaves and serve immediately.

# On fire!

There are a huge number of pepper cultivars available. You can use any cultivars you like, depending on your taste. This selection includes 'Nosegay' and 'Paper Lantern', both with hot, red fruits; 'Sweet Orange Baby', a productive, compact, small-fruited sweet pepper; and 'Healthy', a sweet pepper that will ripen in cooler conditions than most other cultivars.

## Ingredients

1 packet of sweet pepper 'Healthy' seed

1 packet of chili pepper 'Nosegay' seed

1 packet of chili pepper 'Paper Lantern' seed

1 packet of sweet pepper 'Sweet Orange Baby' seed

plastic pots, 3 in. (7.5 cm) in diameter

seed-starter mix

1 terra-cotta bowl planter,
    18 x 12 in. (45 x 30 cm)

all-purpose soil-less mix

drainage material (see page 16)

1 lemon grass plant (*Cymbopogon citratus*)

1 plain terra-cotta pot,
    10 x 12 in. (25 x 30 cm)

2 coriander plants (*Coriandrum sativum*)

1 savory plant (*Satureja spicigera*)

1 terra-cotta bowl, 14 x 9 in. (35 x 23 cm)

1 bag of reddish-brown pebbles

## Method

**1** Sow the peppers in seed-starter mix in small pots in mid-spring, two seeds to a pot, and put them in a heated propagating case or greenhouse. Keep well watered but not too wet. If both the seeds in a pot germinate, pull out the weaker seedling.

**2** When they are growing strongly and all danger of frost has passed, plant the strongest pepper plants—one of each cultivar—into a wide terra-cotta bowl filled with soil-less mix. Follow the instructions for planting a container on page 16. Firm and water well. Pot up the lemon grass in the tall terra-cotta pot and the coriander and savory together in the smaller terra-cotta bowl in the same way. Mulch the containers with a layer of reddish-brown pebbles.

**3** Group the pots together in as sunny a position as possible to encourage a good crop of peppers and to help them ripen as quickly as possible.

---

### Spicy tomato salsa

Finely chop 1 small red onion and 1 garlic clove. Skin, deseed, and chop 1 lb. (500 g) sweet ripe tomatoes. Deseed and finely chop 2 red chilies. Put the onion, garlic, tomatoes, and chilies into a bowl and add 3 tablespoons of finely chopped coriander, 1 tablespoon of lime juice, and 3 tablespoons of olive oil. Season with a pinch of sugar and salt and mix lightly. Cover and chill for 30–60 minutes.

---

# Potato paradise

Potatoes are easy to grow in containers, and even a pot 12 in. (30 cm) across with a single tuber will give a good crop. Although you can grow any potato in a pot, the best for containers are salad types, such as 'French Fingerling', which will give a high yield of small, well-formed, slender tubers.

## Ingredients

9 tubers of salad potato 'French Fingerling'

1 slatted wooden container, 24 x 24 in. (60 x 60 cm)

all-purpose soil-less mix

1 hyssop plant (*Hyssopus officinalis*)

1 thyme plant (*Thymus* 'Peter Davis')

1 Moroccan mint plant (*Mentha spicata* var. *crispa* 'Moroccan')

1 peppermint plant (*Mentha* x *piperita*)

1 parsley plant (*Petroselinum crispum*)

4 plain terra-cotta pots of varying sizes

horticultural grit

high-potash fertilizer

## Method

1 Plant the potatoes, evenly spaced, toward the bottom of a large container that is at least 14 in. (35 cm) deep and cover with a 2–4 in. (5–10 cm) layer of all-purpose soil-less mix.

2 When the potatoes are growing strongly, fill around them with more soil mix. Do this two or three times, as they grow.

3 Team up the hyssop and thyme in the largest pot and plant the mints and parsley individually. Following the instructions for planting a container on page 16, plant them in a soil-less mix with added grit to improve the drainage.

4 Do not overwater the potatoes because potato blight is more prevalent in wet conditions. Feed with a high-potash fertilizer and harvest when the plants have flowered and are beginning to die down.

### Fried warm new potatoes with fresh mint dressing

Cut 1½ lb. (750 g) small new potatoes in half lengthwise and cook them in a hot frying pan for 6 minutes on each side. Meanwhile, mix the finely grated rind and juice of 2 limes with 8 tablespoons grapeseed oil. Season to taste and add 2 tablespoons chopped fresh mint. Toss the potatoes in the dressing and serve garnished with extra mint leaves.

# Peas and beans

As they require the same fertile, moisture-retentive but free-draining conditions, peas and beans make good bedfellows. 'Borlotto Firetongue' is a dwarf French bean with pods that are streaked pinkish red and green, while 'Ferrari', with its plain green pods, is one of the smallest of all French beans. Center stage is given to a group of sprawling asparagus peas. Their chief attraction is their small red flowers that are followed by small, edible winged pods.

## Ingredients

1 packet of dwarf French bean 'Ferrari' seed

1 packet of dwarf French bean 'Borlotto Firetongue' (or a similar cultivar) seed

1 packet of asparagus pea seed (*Lotus tetragonolobus*)

biodegradable peat pots

seed-starter mix

1 wooden window box, 28 x 10 in. (70 x 25 cm)

drainage material (see page 16)

all-purpose soil-less mix

6–8 thin sticks, about 18 in. (45 cm) long, for support

## Method

**1** Sow the beans and asparagus peas in seed-starter mix in individual peat pots to prevent root disturbance when transplanting in the window box, and put them in a heated propagating case or greenhouse to germinate.

**2** Make sure there are plenty of drainage holes in the bottom of the window box, and drill extra ones if necessary. Put a layer of drainage material in the bottom and fill with all-purpose soil-less mix.

**3** Place the seven or eight evenly spaced 'Borlotto Firetongue' plants in a row toward the back of the window box. In the front row plant three asparagus peas spaced 8 in. (20 cm) apart, one dead center, the others on either side. Finally, plant two evenly spaced 'Ferrari' beans between the asparagus peas. Push in a few sticks to help support the plants as they grow.

### French bean and tomato salad

Cook 8 oz. (250 g) French beans. Then cut in half 8 oz. (250 g) mixed red and yellow baby tomatoes. Put the beans and tomatoes in a bowl and mix in a handful of chopped mint, 1 chopped garlic clove, 4 tablespoons olive oil, and 1 tablespoon balsamic vinegar. Season to taste and serve warm or cold.

# Pretty in purple

Handsome-looking eggplant 'Baby Rosanna' bears heavy crops of small but tasty purple fruits. An underplanting of evergreen tricolored sage, with pink, cream, and green aromatic leaves that can be used in the same way as common sage, is the perfect foil. Interspersed with the sage are pink- and blue-flowered annual clary sage, whose leaves can also be used for flavoring.

## Ingredients

1 'Baby Rosanna' eggplant plant
    (or similar small-fruited variety) or
    a packet of seed

cell-pack trays

seed-starter mix

1 packet of annual clary sage
    (*Salvia viridis*) seed

plastic pots, 3 in. (7.5 cm) in diameter

1 gray slate container,
    15 x 15 in. (38 x 38 cm)

drainage material (see page 16)

all-purpose soil-less mix

4 tricolored sage plants
    (*Salvia officinalis* 'Tricolor')

high-potash fertilizer

## Method

**1** Sow the eggplant seed in seed-starter mix in cell-pack trays in a heated propagating case in mid-spring, and the faster maturing annual clary sage in a cold frame a few weeks later. Repot the eggplant seedlings in small individual pots once they are large enough.

**2** Add a layer of drainage material to the bottom of the slate container before filling with soil-less mix. When all danger of frost has passed, plant the strongest, bushiest eggplant (or a bought plant) in the center. Position one of the tricolored sages at each corner and fill in empty space with annual clary sage seedlings.

**3** Pinch out the clary sage to make the plants bush out and trim off the flowering stems as they fade. Feed the eggplant regularly with a high-potash fertilizer.

### Eggplant and yogurt tortillas

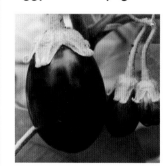

Thinly slice an eggplant and cook in 4 tablespoons olive oil for about 10 minutes. Chop a handful of mint and of parsley and mix with 2 tablespoons chopped chives and 1 seeded and sliced green chili. Add to 7 fl oz. (200 ml) Greek yogurt and 2 tablespoons mayonnaise. Arrange eggplant slices on 2 large tortillas and spread the yogurt mixture over the top. Top with cucumber slices and sprinkle with paprika.

# Roots and shoots

Kohlrabi is a fast-growing, easy plant, and the turniplike stems should be harvested when they reach the size of golf balls. Being shallow-rooted, drought-tolerant creeping thymes offer little competition for water and nutrients, while their tiny green and-golden-yellow leaves provide the perfect accompaniment to the dramatic-looking kohlrabi.

## Ingredients

1 packet of mixed purple and white
  kohlrabi seed

cell-pack trays

seed-starter mix

plastic pots, 3 in. (7.5 cm) in diameter

1 terra-cotta planter,
  20 x 12 in. (50 x 30 cm)

drainage material (see page 16)

all-purpose soil-less mix

6 'Goldstream' thyme plants
  (*Thymus serpyllum*) (non-edible)

## Method

1 Sow the kohlrabi in seed-starter mix in cell-pack trays, two or three seeds to a compartment. When they have germinated, remove the weakest seedlings to let the strongest develop. Once they are large enough, place the best seedlings into small individual pots.

2 Add a layer of drainage material to the bottom of the planter and fill with soil-less mix. Select an even number of purple and white plants—the purple plants have darker stems—and plant them 4 in. (10 cm) apart, alternately through the center of the planter.

3 Carefully split each of the thyme plants into two equal-sized pieces and plant them around the kohlrabi. They will quickly knit together to form a carpet of green and golden-yellow leaves.

### Minty carrot and kohlrabi salad

Mix together 1 tablespoon soft brown sugar, ½ teaspoon sea salt, 8 oz. (250 g) thinly sliced carrots, 5 oz. (150 g) thinly sliced kohlrabi, 7 fl. oz. (200 ml) water and 2½ fl. oz. (65 ml) white wine vinegar. Transfer to the refrigerator for about 1 hour, stirring occasionally. Drain the vegetables and rinse in water. Mix in 2 tablespoons chopped mint leaves and 2 tablespoons chopped fresh coriander leaves, and serve.

# Red devil

This simple but highly effective planting will carry your edible container display well into the cooler, darker months, providing an invaluable supply of leaves for winter use. Radicchio forms tight, succulent heads of glossy leaves that, in most varieties, are green at first, becoming increasingly flushed with red or bronze as they mature. Rising up in the center of the container, ruby-red chard creates a colorful display of glowing red stems and red-veined leaves.

## Ingredients

1 packet of radicchio seed

1 packet of red-stemmed chard or leaf beet seed

seed-starter mix

cell-pack trays

1 old galvanized bucket, 16 x 10 in. (40 x 25 cm)

drainage material (see page 16)

all-purpose soil-less mix

## Method

**1** Sow the radicchio and chard in seed-starter mix in cell-pack trays. Place them in a cold frame to germinate and keep them moist but not too wet.

**2** Drill holes in the bottom of the bucket for drainage, while wearing goggles to protect your eyes from metal splinters. Place a layer of drainage material in the bottom and fill with all-purpose soil-less mix.

**3** Once they are large enough to handle, plant the seedlings in the container, positioning a single chard plant in the center surrounded by four radicchio plants. Keep well watered, and place in a cool but well-lit spot to prevent the plants from bolting to seed prematurely.

---

### Chard and garbanzo bean tortilla

Heat 4 tablespoons of olive oil in a large frying pan. Add 1 chopped onion, 4 crushed garlic cloves, and ½ teaspoon dried chili flakes and fry gently for 10 minutes. Stir in 1 lb. (500 g) shredded chard and 13 oz. (400 g) canned garbanzo beans and cook gently for 5 minutes. Beat 6 eggs in a bowl and season with salt and pepper. Stir in the chard mixture. Wipe out the frying pan and add 4 tablespoons of olive oil. Pour in the chard/egg mixture and cook over a low heat for 10 minutes. Place the tortilla onto a plate, invert the pan over the plate and flip it back in the pan. Return to the heat for 5 minutes until the tortilla is cooked through.

# Pepper pot

This fiery concoction combines edible fruits, flowers, and leaves to create a sizzling display that will last all summer. The tall pot raises the plants closer to eye level where this simple but productive planting can be more readily appreciated. The sweet pepper 'Redskin' is a compact cultivar, producing good-sized fruits that turn from green to glistening red as they ripen.

## Ingredients

1 pale gray, tapered, terrazzo, reconstituted-stone container, 14 x 28 in. (35 x 70 cm)

drainage material (see page 16)

all-purpose soil-less mix

1 'Redskin' sweet pepper plant

4 'Red Wonder' nasturtium plants (*Tropaeolum majus*)

4 Million Bells Crackling Fire plants (*Calibrachoa* 'Sunbelfire') (non-edible)

high-potash fertilizer

## Method

1 Make sure there are plenty of drainage holes in the bottom of the container and, if not, carefully drill a few extra ones. Add a layer of drainage material in the bottom and fill with soil-less mix.

2 Once all danger of frost has passed, plant the pepper in the center of the comtainer, surrounded by nasturtiums and then million bells to trail over and soften the edges of the pot.

3 Harvest the peppers as they ripen and apply a high-potash fertilizer to encourage repeat crops. Deadhead the nasturtiums to keep them flowering well and keep an eye out for predator aphids.

---

### Chicken and sweet pepper kebabs

Cut 8 boneless chicken thighs, 1 onion, 1 red pepper, and 1 green pepper into chunks of the same size. Mix together ¼ pint (150 ml) plain yogurt, 2 tablespoons olive oil, 2 crushed garlic cloves, 2 tablespoons chopped fresh coriander, and 2 tablespoons ground cumin. Stir in the chicken and refrigerate for about an hour. Thread the chicken, onion and peppers on skewers and cook under a hot broiler for 20 minutes, turning frequently. Serve immediately.

# Purple and bronze

Bronze fennel and purplish-pink flowered marjoram alternate at the back of this large, deep, galvanized steel planter to create a tactile backdrop to the bronze-leaved para cress. The graceful fennel, with its aniseed-flavored foliage, can grow to 5 ft. (1.5 m) tall, and it will self-sow if you allow the flowers to set seed. The marjoram has leaves that are purple-hued in spring. The yellow-bronze blooms of the para cress echo the coloring of the fennel leaves.

## Ingredients

1 packet of para cress
 (*Acmella oleracea*) seed

cell-pack trays

seed-starter mix

plastic pots, 3 in. (7.5 cm) in diameter

1 galvanized steel planter,
 24 x 12 in. (60 x 30 cm)

drainage material (see page 16)

all-purpose soil-less mix

3 bronze fennel (*Foeniculum vulgare*
 'Purpureum') plants

2 'Herrenhausen' marjoram plants
 (*Origanum laevigatum*)

## Method

**1** Sow the para cress in seed starter-mix in cell-pack trays in spring. Transfer them to a cold frame to germinate and transplant the seedlings into individual pots when they are large enough to handle.

**2** Add a layer of drainage material to the bottom of the planter and fill with soil-less mix. Plant three strong, bushy fennel plants and two equal-sized marjorams in a row along the back of the container, alternating between the fennel and the marjoram.

**3** Transplant the para cress plantlets to the front of the planter and water well. Pinch out the young leaves and shoot tips and use them in salads.

### Tabbouleh and fennel salad

Prepare 8 oz. (250 g) bulgar wheat according to the directions on the packet, then pour it into a large bowl. Stir in 1 finely sliced fennel bulb, 1 finely sliced red onion, 5 tablespoons chopped mint, 5 tablespoons chopped parsley, 2 tablespoons crushed fennel seeds, 2 tablespoons olive oil, the finely grated rind of 2 lemons and the juice of 1 lemon. Season with salt and pepper, let stand for 30 minutes, then serve with more lemon juice if desired.

# A taste of the Mediterranean

Taking center stage in this terracotta pot is a mini-standard olive tree that, given plenty of warmth, will produce a small but invaluable crop. Its gray-green leaves are an attractive contrast to an underplanting of cut-leaf arugula and bright green-leaved sweet basil.

## Ingredients

1 plain terra-cotta pot,
   17 x 14 in. (42 x 35 cm)

drainage material (see page 16)

soil-based potting mix

all-purpose soil-less mix

1 mini-standard olive
   (*Olea europea*) plant

3 sweet basil (*Ocimum basilicum*) plants

1 packet of cut-leaf annual arugula
   (*Eruca vesicaria*) seed

## Method

1  Add a layer of drainage material to the base of the pot and quarter-fill the container with a half-and-half mix of soil-based and soil-less mix. Set the olive in the center, adding or removing soil mix as necessary until the top of the rootball rests 2 in. (5 cm) below the rim of the pot.

2  Fill in with more soil mix and plant three sweet basils evenly spaced around the olive. Sow the arugula seed direct on to the surface of the soil mix between the basils, and cover lightly.

3  Ensure that the soil mix is kept moist but not too wet, and position the pot in a sunny but sheltered spot. The basils and arugula are annuals; but, if it is overwintered in a frost-free place, the olive tree can be kept from year to year and repotted into a larger container as necessary.

### Simple ciabatta salad

Tear 4 slices of ciabatta bread into pieces and put them in a bowl. Cut 4 tomatoes, ½ cucumber, and 1 red onion into similar-sized pieces and add them to the bowl. Mix in a handful of chopped flat leaf parsley and 1 tablespoon chopped black olives. In a separate bowl, mix 4 tablespoons olive oil, 1–2 tablespoons wine vinegar, and 2 tablespoons lemon juice. Pour the dressing over the salad and let to stand for 1 hour at room temperature before serving.

# Kale and cabbage

Cabbage does best in fairly cool conditions. Red cabbage in particular is usually grown for picking in late summer to autumn. Here the cultivar 'Red Jewel' is planted in a triangle amid a sea of 'Dwarf Green Curled' kale in a large rough-cast, mellow stone-effect concrete container.

## Ingredients

1 packet of red cabbage (such as 'Red Jewel') seed

1 packet of compact-growing green kale (such as 'Dwarf Green Curled') seed

cell-pack trays

seed-starter mix

1 stone-effect concrete container, 16 x 14 in. (40 x 35 cm)

drainage material (see page 16)

all-purpose soil-less mix

## Method

1 Sow the cabbage and kale in seed-starter mix in cell-pack trays in early spring for a summer crop or in early summer for winter harvesting. Transfer to a cold frame to germinate.

2 When they are large enough to handle and growing strongly, plant them out in a large container, following the instructions for planting a container on page 16. Set three cabbages in a triangle formation with the kale filling the gaps in between. Plant the kale fairly close together so that it can be thinned out, and the thinnings used as baby leaves in salads.

3 Let some kale mature to use later in the season and to keep the display looking good. Keep an eye out for caterpillars at all times, because they can eat their way through a crop in hours. Small numbers can be simply picked off.

### Cabbage with bacon

Fry 1 sliced onion, 1 crushed garlic clove, 1 diced red chili, and 4 oz. (125 g) diced bacon in 1 tablespoon olive oil until soft. Cut 1 head of cabbage in half lengthwise, discard the hard central stem and roughly chop the leaves. Add to the onion mixture with 3 fl. oz. (75 ml) chicken stock, stir well, season with salt and pepper and cook for 4 minutes. Sprinkle 3 oz. (75 g) grated Parmesan cheese and 2 tablespoons chopped parsley over the top and serve immediately.

# On the bay

This aromatic gathering of evergreen culinary herbs will provide a year-round display. When planted in a wooden Versailles-style container and clipped as a topiary lollipop, sweet bay forms a classic centerpiece. The accompanying terra-cotta pots are filled with violet-flowered rosemary and scented-leaf geraniums.

## Ingredients

1 quarter-standard sweet bay (*Laurus nobilis*), clipped as a lollipop

1 square wooden Versailles planter, 16 x 16 in. (40 x 40 cm)

drainage material (see page 16)

all-purpose soil-less mix

soil-based potting mix

1 'Severn Sea' rosemary plant (*Rosmarinus officinalis*)

2 different scented-leaved geraniums (as available)

3 plain round terra-cotta pots in an assortment of sizes, 6–10 in. (15–25 cm) across

1 bag black, river-polished pebbles

## Method

**1** Choose a straight-stemmed, quarter-standard bay lollipop from your local nursery or garden center. It may be expensive but it will last for years given winter protection.

**2** Add a layer of drainage material to the bottom of a Versailles planter and plant the bay in the container using a half-and-half mix of soil-less and soil-based mixes. In the same way, pot the rosemary and geraniums in individual terra-cotta pots, this time using soil-less mix.

**3** Group the pots together to create a pleasing composition and mulch the surface of the Versailles planter with black polished pebbles for a contemporary look. Trim the bay two or three times throughout the season to keep its shape, and trim the rosemary after flowering.

### Sea bass baked in a packet

Mix the rind from 2 oranges with 2 tablespoons olive oil. Slice the orange flesh and arrange half the slices on 4 large rectangles of wax paper. Place the sea bass on the slices and insert a bay leaf in each cavity and 1 on top. Put the remaining orange slices on top. Drizzle with the oil and rind mixture, fold the paper around the fish and bake in a preheated oven, at 375°F (190°C), for 20 minutes.

# Fireball

These dwarf chili peppers are perfectly happy growing in a large hanging basket, where they create an explosion of fiery color in mid- to late summer. The centerpiece is the reliable 'Apache', which is crowded with small tapered fruits that turn from rich, glossy green to a startling bright red.

## Ingredients

1 'Apache' chili pepper plant

4 'Prairie Fire' chili pepper plants
(or similar dwarf cultivar) or
1 packet of seed

plastic pots, 3 in. (7.5 cm) (optional)

seed-starter mix (optional)

1 willow or rattan hanging basket,
14 in. (35 cm) across

plastic liner

all-purpose soil-less mix

4 parrot's beak plants
(*Lotus maculatus* x *berhelottii*)
(non-edible)

## Method

**1** If you are growing them from seed, sow the chili peppers in seed-starter mix in small individual pots in mid-spring, two seeds to a pot, and put them in a heated propagating case or greenhouse. Keep well watered but not too wet. If both seeds germinate, pull out the weaker seedling.

**2** Choose a large willow or rattan closed-sided hanging basket and pierce several holes in the bottom of the plastic lining. Fill with a good-quality, soil-less mix.

**3** Plant the 'Apache' chili in the center with the plants of the other cultivars spaced evenly around it. Fill in the gaps with the parrot's beak plants. Fill around the plants with more soil-less mix and water well.

**4** Stand the basket on a pot and leave it in a greenhouse to settle for a few weeks before you hang it in its final position, once all danger of frost has passed. Choose as sunny a position as possible to make sure that you get a good crop of colorful fruits.

### Chicken with chili jam

Put 4 oz. (125 g) deseeded and chopped chilies, 1 crushed garlic clove, 1 chopped onion, 2 in. (5 cm) chopped ginger root, 4 fl. oz. (125 ml) vinegar, and 1 lb. (500 g) sugar into a saucepan, bring to a boil, then simmer for 15 minutes until it becomes thick and jamlike. Meanwhile heat a frying pan. Cook 4 chicken breasts in the pan, skin-side down, for 10 minutes on each. Serve the chicken with the chili jam over the top.

# Green garnish

This delightful container presents a selection of the most useful garnishing herbs. Parsley is a hardy biennial forming mounds of fresh-green leaves, while coriander is grown both for its leaves and the seeds that follow the tiny white summer flowers. Arugula is a favorite Mediterranean garnish and the long flat leaves of Chinese chives add a garlic flavoring when sprinkled over dishes.

## Ingredients

1 metal bucket, 14 x 8 in. (35 x 20 cm)

drainage material (see page 16)

all-purpose soil-less mix

2 annual arugula
  (*Eruca vesicaria*) plants

1 parsley (*Petroselinum crispum*) plant

1 garlic or Chinese chives (*Allium tuberosum*) plant

1 coriander (*Coriandrum sativum*) plant

## Method

**1** Turn the bucket upside down and drill holes in the bottom for drainage. Wear goggles to protect your eyes from metal splinters.

**2** Add a layer of drainage material in the bottom and half-fill the container with all-purpose soil-less mix.

**3** Position the plants, placing the shorter-growing arugula toward the front, with the medium-growing parsley and chives to each side, and the tall-growing coriander at the back. Fill in with more soil mix, firm gently and water well. Pick regularly to encourage lots of new leaves.

### Spiced couscous salad

Combine 7 fl. oz. (200 ml) vegetable stock with 7 fl. oz. (200 ml) orange juice, 1 teaspoon ground cinnamon, ½ teaspoon ground coriander, and ½ teaspoon salt in a saucepan. Bring it to the boil, stir in 8 oz. (250 g) couscous and remove the pan from the heat. Cover and let stand for 10 minutes. Combine 3 oz. (75 g) raisins, ½ bunch of roughly chopped parsley, ½ bunch of roughly chopped mint, 1 crushed garlic clove and 4 tablespoons of oil in a bowl. Stir in the soaked couscous, and season with salt and pepper.

# Lots of leaves

Chinese cabbage 'Santo' and radicchio 'Palla Rossa Red Devil' give a display of shaped and textured leaves that is shown off to perfection in an earthenware container. Both can be left to mature and be harvested as whole heads, or you can pick a few leaves at a time. In a container, however, they are best planted more closely than in the ground, harvested when young, and replaced with another crop.

## Ingredients

1 packet of Chinese cabbage (such as 'Santo') seed

1 packet of radicchio (such as 'Palla Rossa Red Devil') seed

cell-pack trays (optional)

seed-starter mix (optional)

1 earthenware container, 16 x 18 in. (40 x 45 cm)

drainage material (see page 16)

all-purpose soil-less mix

## Method

**1** Sow the Chinese cabbage and radicchio in seed-starter mix in cell-pack trays in summer, for harvesting in autumn. Alternatively, sow directly into the container and thin out as necessary.

**2** Cell-pack-raised plants should be carefully transplanted as soon as they are strong enough to handle. Following the instructions for planting a container on page 16, transplant into all-purpose soil-less mix, positioning a block of Chinese cabbages in the center with a ring of radicchio to surround them.

**3** Position the container in a sunny but not too hot position, because too much heat may cause them to bolt to seed. Keep the plants well watered and watch out for predator snails and caterpillars.

---

### Radicchio with pears and Stilton

Cut 4 pears into quarters and arrange them in a single layer on a sheet of aluminum foil, turning up the edges. Mix together the juice and grated rind of 2 oranges and 4 tablespoons clear honey. Pour the mixture over the pears and press the edges of the foil together to seal. Transfer to a frying pan and cook over a moderate heat for 15–20 minutes. Meanwhile, cut 4 small heads of radicchio into quarters, brush with walnut oil and cook under a grill for 2–3 minutes on each side. Arrange the pears and juices on plates with the radicchio, and crumble over 4 oz. (125 g) Stilton cheese.

# Desserts

An apple a day **112**

Blueberry surprise **114**

Lemon zest **116**

Strawberry ball **118**

Gorgeous grapes **120**

Currant affair **122**

Mellow yellow **124**

Tea pot **126**

Pop and go **128**

Gorgeous gourds **130**

Pear delight **132**

Passion fashion **134**

# An apple a day

*begonias only*

Apples grown on a dwarf or very dwarf rootstock will grow to about 6 ft. (1.8 m) tall after 10 years or so and are ideal for containers. When grown in a generous-sized container and fed with a high-potash fertilizer from blossom time until shortly before harvest, they will produce a worthwhile crop.

## Ingredients

1 wooden half-barrel,
   28 x 16 in. (70 x 40 cm)

drainage material (see page 16)

soil-based potting mix

all-purpose soil-less mix

1 apple on a very dwarf rootstock
   (such as M27)

wooden stake (optional)

8 begonia 'Non Stop Appleblossom'
   plants

## Method

1  Choose a large wooden half-barrel and place it in a sunny but sheltered position. Once planted, the container will be heavy and difficult to move, so make sure it is in exactly the right spot and plant it on site.

2  Put a layer of drainage material in the bottom of the container and add a layer of a half-and-half mix of soil-less and soil-based mixes. Position the apple tree in the center and fill in with more soil mix, firming gently. The roots of dwarf apple trees are generally fairly shallow and compact so it may be necessary to provide a wooden stake for support in exposed locations.

3  Plant a ring of begonias around the tree. In future years the roots of the apple will prevent replanting at its base, but you could sprinkle seeds of hardy annuals on the surface of the soil mix, because they will offer minimal root competition.

### Apple tartlets with passion fruit cream

Cut 4 circles, ¼ inch (5 mm) thick, from 8 oz. (250 g) puff pastry. Put them on a greased baking sheet and prick. Peel, core and slice 3 apples and arrange the slices on the pastry. Drizzle with 1 oz. (25 g) melted butter and sprinkle with 3½ oz. (100 g) sugar. Cook in a preheated oven, at 400°F (200°C), for 15–20 minutes. Mix the flesh of 2–3 passionfruit with 4 fl. oz. (125 ml) cream and serve with the apple tartlets.

# Blueberry surprise

Not only do blueberries produce heavy crops of delicious fruits, they also offer great visual appeal. In spring they produce sweetly scented, creamy white flowers; in summer the dark blue fruits appear; and in autumn the leaves turn shades of gold and red before they fall. Cranberries enjoy the same acidic soil conditions and because of their low and trailing habit are excellent for underplanting blueberries.

## Ingredients

drainage material (see page 16)

1 dark blue-green, round, glazed container, 20 x 18 in. (50 x 45 cm)

ericaceous acidic soil mix

1 'Elliott' blueberry plant (*Vaccinium corymbosum*)

3 cranberry (*Vaccinium oxycoccos*) plants

1 bag of cocoa shells

ericaceous fertilizer

## Method

**1** Put a layer of drainage material in the bottom of the container and half-fill it with ericaceous soil mix.

**2** Place the blueberry in the center of the pot so that the top of its rootball rests 3 in. (8 cm) below the rim of the pot. Evenly space the cranberries around it, allowing their stems to trail over the edges.

**3** Fill in with more soil mix and firm gently. Water well and mulch with cocoa shells. Water with rainwater, if possible, and feed occasionally during the growing season with an ericaceous fertilizer. If necessary, prune the cranberries during spring.

---

### Blueberry and mascarpone gratin

Arrange 2 oz. (50 g) blueberries on 2 ovenproof plates or in gratin dishes. Beat together 2 oz. (50 g) mascarpone cheese, 1 egg yolk, 1 oz. (25 g) sugar, and 1 tablespoon Amaretto di Saronno. Spoon the smooth mixture over the fruits and cook under a hot broiler for about 3 minutes, until the sauce is caramelized and the fruits have softened.

---

# Lemon zest

When underplanted with scented geraniums and accompanied by a billowing pot of tangerine sage, this fruiting lemon tree creates not only a visual feast but also a treat for the nostrils and tastebuds. The variety 'Meyer' is a compact hybrid that bears fragrant white flowers from spring to summer, followed by small but well-formed fruits. Keep the container outdoors on a sunny patio in summer but move to a frost-free spot in winter.

## Ingredients

1 'Meyer' lemon plant (*Citrus x meyeri*)

1 cylindrical terra-cotta pot,
   16 x 16 in. (40 x 40 cm)

drainage material (see page 16)

soil-based potting mix

all-purpose soil-less mix

3 scented-leaved geranium plants
   (lemon-scented if possible)

1 tangerine sage plant (*Salvia elegans*)
   (non-edible)

1 cylindrical terra-cotta pot,
   12 x 12 in. (30 x 30 cm)

## Method

**1** Pot the lemon in the larger container, placing a layer of drainage material in the bottom. Use a half-and-half mix of soil-based and soil-less mixes.

**2** Position the three geraniums evenly around the lemon, placing them toward the edge of the pot. Fill in with more soil mix.

**3** Plant the tangerine sage in the smaller pot. Remove faded flowers from the geraniums. While it is in an actively growing stage, feed the lemon tree every two to three weeks.

### Lemon and cinnamon pancakes

Sift 4 oz. (125 g) all-purpose flour, ½ teaspoon ground cinnamon, a pinch of salt and 1 teaspoon lemon rind into a bowl. Gradually beat in 1 egg, ½ pint (300 ml) milk and ½ oz. (15 g) melted butter to make a smooth batter. Brush a small frying pan with a little oil and fry a ladleful of batter for a minute before flipping the pancake over. Continue until all the batter is used. Serve 2–3 pancakes per person.

# Strawberry ball

Strawberries are among the easiest of all fruits to grow in containers. Fed and watered well, they will thrive even within the confines of a hanging basket. Indeed, growing strawberries so that they are raised off the ground makes them less accessible to slugs and snails. Choose a perpetual or everbearing cultivar, such as 'Ogalalla', which will provide a supply of succulent fruits from early summer right through to the fall.

## Ingredients

1 open-sided, wire or plastic hanging basket, 14 in. (35 cm) across

1 hanging basket liner suitable for a 14 in. (35 cm) basket

all-purpose soil-less mix

9 perpetually fruiting strawberry plants, such as 'Ogalalla'

netting (optional)

high-potash fertilizer

## Method

1 Line the hanging basket with a flexible liner such as coconut fiber matting or a synthetic moss substitute and fill with soil-less mix to a third of its depth.

2 Choose nine healthy, virus-free, young strawberry plants and carefully push four of them through the side of the basket, about halfway up, making holes in the lining to do so.

3 Add more soil mix and plant up more strawberries in the top of the basket. Use one plant in the center and the remaining four spaced alternately to those in the layer below. If necessary, cover with netting to protect from birds. Water regularly and feed weekly with a high-potash fertilizer.

### Fruit skewers dipped in chocolate sauce

Break 2 oz. (50 g) milk chocolate and 3 oz. (75 g) dark chocolate into small pieces and put them in a pan with 3 fl. oz. (75 ml) milk and 2 teaspoons light molasses. Heat gently, stirring, until melted and smooth. Meanwhile, cut 1 red-skinned apple, 2 peaches, 1 kiwifruit, 8 oz. (250 g) strawberries, and 1 banana into bite-size chunks to dip into the warm sauce.

# Gorgeous grapes

Confined in a container, where they will grow less vigorously, grapevines make handsome specimens, their leaves turning to fiery shades in autumn. This gnarled-stemmed standard grapevine is underplanted with bugleweed, the colored leaves of which, although edible, are unpalatable so are used here purely for their ornamental appeal.

## Ingredients

1 earthenware container,
  20 x 16 in. (50 x 40 cm)

drainage material (see page 16)

1 standard grape vine 'New York
  Muscat' or similar dessert variety
  (*Vitis vinifera*)

soil-based potting mix

all-purpose soil-less mix

horticultural grit

3 bugleweed 'Braunherz' plants
  (or similar bronze-leaved cultivar)
  (*Ajuga reptans*)

3 bugleweed 'Golden Beauty' plants
  (or similar variegated-leaf cultivar)
  (*Ajuga reptans*)

## Method

1 Position the container in a warm, sunny spot, preferably near a wall where the grapes can bask in the reflected heat. Vines do not do well in wet conditions, so place a deep layer of drainage material in the bottom of the container. Pot the vine using a half-and-half mix of soil-based and soil-less mixes with added grit to keep the soil open and free draining.

2 Plant the bugleweed plants around the edge of the pot so that they will both creep inwards as well as tumble over the edge.

3 During the growing season, feed the vine every two to three weeks. Spray as necessary to discourage mildew and other fungal problems, and prune to restrict growth during summer and winter to encourage a compact framework and plenty of fruiting spurs.

### Lemon posset with frosted grapes

Gently heat ½ pint (300 ml) heavy cream, 3 oz. (75 g) sugar and the grated rind of ½ lemon until the sugar has dissolved. Simmer until the cream bubbles around the edges. Remove from the heat and add 4 tablespoons lemon juice. Pour into 4 dishes and chill for 4 hours. Dip 5 oz. (150 g) grapes, snipped into small bunches, in beaten egg white and then coat with sugar. Serve on top of the chilled dessert.

# Currant affair

Red currants are among the most ornamental of all soft fruits with their glistening red fruits hanging conspicuously in long strings. For a truly striking display, team red currant 'Cascade' with an underplanting of powerfully perfumed 'Raspberry Sundae' garden pinks, whose petals are also edible. 'Cascade' is an early to mid-season currant cultivar that matures over a long period, producing small, slightly acidic fruits.

## Ingredients

1 charcoal-gray, square, terrazzo, reconstituted-stone container, 16 x 16 in. (40 x 40 cm)

drainage material (see page 16)

soil-based potting mix

all-purpose soil-less mix

1 red currant 'Cascade' plant or similar smaller variety

8 'Raspberry Sundae' garden pink plants (*Dianthus*) (or similar dwarf variety)

## Method

1 Put a layer of drainage material in the bottom of the container and fill with a half-and-half mix of soil-based and soil-less mixes. Plant the red currant in the center of the container and position the garden pinks symmetrically around it.

2 Remove faded flowers from the garden pinks regularly and, after the 'Cascade' produces flowers and fruit, move the pot to a less prominent position. Transplant the garden pinks to a sunny, well-drained spot in the garden.

3 Cut back all sideshoots produced by the red currant during the growing season to four or five leaves from their base in early summer. Feed regularly while the fruit is developing.

---

### Summer berry sorbet

Blend 8 oz. (250 g) mixed summer berries, 3 fl. oz. (75 ml) spiced berry cordial, 2 tablespoons Kirsch, and 1 tablespoon lime juice in a food processor, taking care not to make the mixture too smooth. Transfer the sorbet to a chilled plastic container and freeze for at least 25 minutes. Spoon into bowls and serve.

# Mellow yellow

This striking composition comprises a well-matched pairing of red-leaved banana (*Ensete ventricosum* 'Maurelii') and yellow-skinned zucchini. Choose *Musa acuminata* 'Dwarf Cavendish' if you want bananas for eating, but it will not produce fruit if winter temperatures fall below 15°C (59°F).

## Ingredients

1 packet zucchini 'Orelia' seed

biodegradable peat pots

seed-starter mix

1 earthenware container,
  16 x 18 in. (40 x 45 cm)

drainage material (see page 16)

all-purpose soil-less mix

1 banana plant (use *Musa acuminata* 'Dwarf Cavendish' if you want edible fruit or *Ensete ventricosum* 'Maurelii' for purely ornamental appearance)

1 bag of assorted pebbles

## Method

1 In mid- to late spring sow the zucchini seed in seed-starter mix in individual peat pots and place them in a heated greenhouse or propagating case. Once they are large enough, move to a sheltered cold frame and transplant once all danger of frost has passed.

2 Position the container where it will be sheltered from strong winds. Make sure that there are plenty of drainage holes in the bottom of the container and add a layer of drainage material. Fill with a good-quality, soil-less mix and plant the banana at the back of the container.

3 Plant a strong, healthy zucchini plant in front of the banana and cover the exposed soil mix with a layer of pebbles. Feed every couple of weeks during the growing season, and remove damaged and yellowing lower leaves as necessary. Harvest the zucchini when they are about 4–6 in. (10–15 cm) long.

---

### Carrot and zucchini cupcakes

Line a 12-section muffin pan. Put 4 oz. (125 g) butter, 4 oz. (125 g) sugar, 5 oz. (150 g) all-purpose flour, 1 teaspoon baking powder, 1 teaspoon mixed spice, 3 oz. (75 g) ground almonds, 2 eggs, and the rind of half an orange in a mixing bowl and beat until light and creamy. Add 3 oz. (75 g) grated carrots, 3 oz. (75 g) grated zucchini, 2 oz. (50 g) golden raisins and stir in until combined. Divide the mixture evenly in the pan. Bake in a preheated oven, at 350°F (180°C), for 25 minutes until risen. Let cool in the pan.

# Tea pot

This dark green, glazed earthenware pot contains a trio of handsome herbs that provide contrasting textures and aromas. Peppermint is one the most strongly aromatic of all and, in common with lemon verbena, its leaves can be used to make herbal teas and tisanes. Nestling at the front of the pot is Roman chamomile, which forms a mat of fresh leaves, topped in summer by yellow-centered, white daisylike flowers that can be used to make a soothing chamomile tea.

## Ingredients

drainage material (see page 16)

1 octagonal, glazed pot,
  14 x 14 in. (35 x 35 cm)

all-purpose soil-less mix

1 lemon verbena plant (*Aloysia triphylla*)

1 peppermint plant (*Mentha* x *piperita*)

2 plastic pots, 6½ in. (16.25 cm) in diameter

2 Roman chamomile plants (*Chamaemelum nobile*)

## Method

**1** Place a layer of drainage material in the bottom of the octagonal pot and half-fill with good-quality soil-less mix.

**2** Place the lemon verbena and peppermint in individual plastic pots so that they can be plunged into the container separately—the lemon verbena so that it can be lifted and given winter protection, and the peppermint to prevent it from swamping the other plants.

**3** Plunge the potted lemon verbena and peppermint toward the back of the main pot and fill in empty spaces with soil mix. Fill the gap at the front of the pot with the chamomile. If the peppermint gets too large, lift it out, cut it back, split it and repot it. It will quickly regrow, and the freshest, youngest leaves are best for herbal teas.

---

### Chamomile tea

To make 1 cup, put 3 chamomile flowerheads, a small flowering spray of lemon verbena, and a couple of lemon verbena leaves in a cup with 1 teaspoon honey. Add 7 fl oz. (200 ml) boiling water and let it infuse for 4–5 minutes. Don't infuse the herbs for too long, or the tea may become bitter.

---

# Pop and go

The sweet corn cultivar 'Red Strawberry' produces bright red cobs, useful for autumn to winter decoration and for edible popcorn. The sweet corn is underplanted with a carpet of strawberries in a pewter-colored planter. Make sure the container is placed in a sunny position, or the sweet corn will not ripen. To make popcorn, the cobs need to be perfectly ripe and thoroughly dried.

## Ingredients

1 packet 'Red Strawberry' popcorn seed (or similar red cultivar)

plastic pots, 3 in. (7.5 cm) in diameter

seed-starter mix

drainage material (see page 16)

1 pewter-colored, square, zinc planter 16 x 16 in. (40 x 40 cm)

all-purpose soil-less mix

4 perpetualy fruiting strawberry plants (such as 'Tribute')

## Method

1 Sow the popcorn seeds in seed-starter mix in individual pots in spring and place them in a cold frame or greenhouse to germinate and grow on.

2 Once the popcorn plants are large enough to transplant and all danger of frost has passed, add a layer of drainage material to the bottom of the zinc planter and fill with a good-quality, soil-less mix. Select four of the strongest plants and plant them in a square formation.

3 Fill in around the popcorn with young, virus-free strawberry plants. Remove all the flowers that form before early summer so that the strawberries produce a more substantial and prolonged crop later in the season.

---

### Strawberry parfaits

Purée 7 oz. (200 g) strawberries with 4 oz. (125 g) mascarpone cheese and 1 tablespoon finely grated lemon rind and 1 tablespoon lemon juice. Transfer to a bowl. Whip ¼ pint (150 ml) heavy cream with 3 tablespoons sugar, then fold into the purée. Spoon into 4 bowls and chill until ready to serve. Just before serving, decorate with red currants, blueberries, and additional grated lemon rind.

# Gorgeous gourds

Most gourds are edible while they are young and tender, although some are more palatable than others. When left to mature they become ornamental and can be picked and used for indoor decoration. The gourds here are grown to climb up an obelisk of copper pipes, intertwined with a handsome, yellow-leaved golden hop.

## Ingredients

1 packet mixed trailing/climbing gourd or squash seed

plastic pots, 3 in. (7.5 cm) in diameter

seed-starter mix

1 square, bronze-colored, zinc container, 16 x 16 in. (40 x 40 cm)

drainage material (see page 16)

all-purpose soil-less mix

1 golden hop plant (*Humulus lupulus* 'Aureus')

1 metal obelisk, 4 ft. (1.2 m) high

## Method

**1** Sow the gourds in spring in seed-starter mix in individual pots and place them in a heated propagating case or greenhouse to germinate. Alternatively, they can be sown outdoors once all danger of frost has passed.

**2** Add a layer of drainage material to the bottom of the zinc container and fill with all-purpose soil-less mix. Transplant out the hop and three of the strongest, healthiest gourd plants, one at each corner of the pot.

**3** Insert a pyramidal obelisk framework into the soil mix and wind the climbing stems of the hop and gourds in as they grow. You can buy a purchased frame or make your own using copper pipe. Water copiously, feed once a week, and remove yellow or damaged leaves as they appear.

### Squash and ginger ice cream

Cut the flesh of a small squash into pieces, steam for 10–15 minutes until tender, then let cool. Blend the squash with 4 tablespoons lime juice and 2 pieces crystallized ginger. Heat 4 egg yolks and 4 oz. (125 g) light brown sugar in a bowl placed over simmering water and whisk until thick, then fold in the squash purée. Whisk 8 fl. oz. (250 ml) heavy cream into soft peaks and fold into the squash mixture. Freeze overnight.

# Pear delight

*tomatoes only*

When underplanted with striking, red-leaved radicchio and dwarf, yellow-fruited tomatoes, this columnar pear tree makes a worthy centerpiece for any patio, terrace, or courtyard. Although it will crop far better if another pear is planted nearby, 'Concorde' is partly self-fertile and so will produce a respectable crop, even in isolation.

## Ingredients

1 packet of 'Yellow Balconi' tomato seed or 3 plants

seed-starter mix

cell-pack trays

1 packet of 'Palla Rossa Red Devil' radicchio seed

1 plain terra-cotta container, 18 x 20 in. (45 x 50 cm)

drainage material (see page 16)

1 compact column pear 'Concorde' on Quince A rootstock

soil-based potting mix

all-purpose soil-less mix

## Method

1 Sow the tomato seed in seed-starter mix in cell-pack trays in a heated greenhouse or propagating case in early spring or buy young plants in mid- to late spring. Sow the radicchio in seed-starter mix in cell-pack trays in a cold frame from mid- to late spring.

2 Site the container in a sunny, sheltered position. Make sure that there are plenty of drainage holes in the bottom of the container and add a layer of drainage material. Pot the pear using a half-and-half mix of soil-based and soil-less mixes.

3 Once all danger of frost has passed, plant three strong tomato plants— one on each side of the container, toward the edge—and fill in between them with radicchio.

### Poached vanilla pears

Put 1 split vanilla bean and 1 pint (600 ml) vin santo in a saucepan. Stand 6 peeled pears in the saucepan, cover and poach them for about 25 minutes. Allow to cool, then transfer the pears to a serving dish. Scrape the seeds from the vanilla bean and add them to the liquid in the saucepan. Boil to reduce to ½ pint (300 ml). Blend in 2 teaspoons arrowroot dissolved in a little water. Heat and whisk to thicken. Stir in 1 teaspoon vanilla extract. Let cool and pour over the pears.

# Passion fashion

In hot summers, the breathtaking blooms of passion flowers are followed by equally eye-catching fruits, many of which are edible. We've used a particularly decorative cultivar with bright red, cherrylike, sweet-tasting fruits. It has climbed over a hooped bamboo cane at the back of the pot, and is accompanied by dwarf Cape gooseberries.

## Ingredients

1 packet dwarf Cape gooseberry 'Little Lantern' (*Physalis peruviana*) seed or 3 plants

cell-pack trays

seed-starter mix

plastic pots, 6½ in. (16.25 cm) in diameter

1 passion flower plant (*Passiflora foetida* var. *hirsutissima* or *P. edulis*)

1 earthenware pot, 16 x 16 in. (40 x 40 cm)

drainage material (see page 16)

soil-based potting mix

1 hooped bamboo cane support, 24 in. (60 cm) high

## Method

1 Sow the Cape gooseberries in seed-starter mix in cell-pack trays in a heated greenhouse or plant rack in spring. Once germinated, pot the strongest seedlings into individual pots.

2 Once all danger of frost has passed, add a layer of drainage material to the bottom of the container, fill with soil-based mix, and place the passion flower at the back and the Cape gooseberries in a group of three in front.

3 Set the bamboo support at the back of the container and weave the passion flower stems around it. Continue to wind the stems in as they grow. After fruiting, the Cape gooseberry plants should be discarded, but the passion flower can be potted and moved into a frost-free greenhouse.

### Creamy passionfruit and vanilla sodas

Halve 8 passionfruit and scoop the pulp into a food processor or blender. Add 8 scoops of vanilla ice cream and 10 tablespoons vanilla syrup. Blend until smooth. Pour into 4 glasses and top up with soda water. Add another scoop of ice cream to each glass and serve at once, with stirrers.

# What to grow

If you are determined enough, you can persuade just about any edible plant to grow in a container. Some plants positively thrive in pots, hanging baskets, and window boxes, even performing better than those planted in the open ground. Edible plants are easier to manage when they are cultivated in containers, and there are dwarf or compact cultivars that are specially bred for growing in confined spaces. Some vegetables can also be harvested early, before they outgrow their allotted space.

Vegetables **138**
Fruits **148**
Herbs **151**
Edible flowers **156**

# Vegetables

## Edible leaves and stems

**Arugula.** Also known as rucola, roquette, or rocket (*Eruca versicaria*) arugula is an excellent cut-and-come-again crop, providing a supply of spicy, fresh leaves over a long period from spring to early winter. It is a fast-growing, half-hardy annual, 2–3 ft. (60–90 cm) tall. Both the leaves and pale yellow flowers can be used in soups and salads and as a garnish. Sow seed in succession from spring onwards in moisture-retentive, rich soil in partial shade. Leaves can be cut for the table as soon as three weeks after planting. Flea beetles may be a problem, and in hot weather plants often bolt.

**Cabbage.** Larger species of cabbage (*Brassica oleracea* Capitata Group) are not suitable for growing in containers. Choose miniature kinds that form small heads and can be harvested and used before they are fully mature. It is possible to grow different species of cabbage over a long period: Spring cabbages, sown in autumn, can be eaten in spring as loose leaves (spring greens) or when the hearts firm up; summer and autumn cabbages, sown in spring, will mature in four to six months; and winter cabbages, sown in spring, are eaten in winter. Close spacing by sowing at distances of 6–8 in. (15–20 cm), rather than the traditional 10 in. (25 cm) or more, will give heads about 20 in. (8 cm) across. Among the cultivars suitable for this treatment are the early-maturing 'Hispi', the autumn 'Minicole', the Savoy 'Protovoy', and the red cabbage 'Primero'. Cabbages grown in containers need fertile, well-drained, alkaline soil, and regularly require water. Cabbages are susceptible to clubroot and *Brassica* white blister and may be attacked by cabbage root fly, mealy cabbage aphids, and flea beetles. Caterpillars are a serious pest of all *Brassicas*, so be vigilant and pick them off by hand whenever you spot them.

**Cauliflower.** As with cabbages, standard cauliflower species (*Brassica oleracea* Botrytis Group) grow too large and take too long to mature to be an economical use of valuable space in a container. Again, however, there are cultivars that can be planted more closely and harvested when they reach the size of a tennis ball or slightly larger. There are also more colorful, ornamental forms with purple, green, or even orange-tinted curds. Sow seed in cell-pack trays in late spring under cover or in early summer outdoors. Take care when transplanting because cauliflower growth is easily stunted. Cauliflowers need fertile, moisture-retentive, alkaline soil. They will produce small heads, about 3 in. (8 cm) across, when they are set out at distances of about 6 in. (15 cm). Sow seed in succession and each group should crop after about ten weeks. Among the cultivars suitable for close spacing in containers are 'Idol' and 'Candid Charm'. Clubroot is the most serious disease, and cabbage root fly, whitefly and caterpillars can cause problems.

**Endive.** Endive (*Cichorium endivia*) is a relative of chicory and can be harvested throughout much of the year. When treated as a cut-and-come-again crop, the leaves are used in salads and have a slightly bitter taste unless blanched by placing an upturned flower pot over the plants to exclude light. Hardier, broad-leaved endives are used for winter crops and the more decorative curly-leaved (frisee) endives for summer salads. Sow seed under cover in mid-spring or outdoors in early summer for a late summer crop; in summer for an autumn crop; and, if you can protect the plants with cloches, in late summer for a winter crop. Endives do best in fertile, moisture-retentive soil, and they prefer fairly cool conditions. They generally crop 7–13 weeks after sowing. Curly-leaved cultivars include the very hardy 'Green Curled' (or 'Moss Curled'), 'Green Curled Ruffec', 'Kentucky', and 'Sally'. Broad-leaved types include 'Batavian Green', 'Cornet d'Anjou', and 'Eminence'. Slugs and aphids cause the most usual problems.

**Kale.** Kale (*Brassica oleracea* Acephala Group), a relative of cabbage, is grown for the curly edged leaves, which are a useful

| Cabbage | Cauliflower | Rhubarb chard | Endive |

year-round crop, especially in winter. Red-leaved varieties intensify in color as temperatures drop. Sow seed in cell-pack trays under cover in late winter or outdoors in mid- to late spring, transplanting into well-drained soil in full sun. It is possible to harvest leaves of some cultivars seven weeks after sowing. Choose compact varieties or harvest as a cut-and-come-again crop. Seedlings can be cut when they are 2–3 in. (5–8 cm) high and used in salads or the individual leaves picked around 18 weeks from sowing and steamed or stir-fried. Among the best dwarf cultivars are 'Showbor', which has tightly curled leaves; and 'Dwarf Green Curled', which has blue-green curled leaves. If you have a large container try 'Redbor', the tall 'Black Tuscany' ('Nero di Toscana'), 'Darkibor' or 'Pentland Brig'. Kales suffer from the same pests and diseases as cabbages (see page 138).

**Lettuce.** Of all the salad crops, lettuce (*Lactuca sativa*) is one of the easiest to grow in containers. There is a wide range of leaf shapes, colors, textures, and flavors, The frilly and red-leaved kinds are particularly decorative. Nonhearting, loose-leaf types are ideal for containers because they can be picked a few leaves at a time rather than harvested whole. Given the protection of cloches during the colder months, they can be grown virtually year round and are a useful crop for combining with spring bulbs in containers. Sow seed successively from late winter (under cover) to early autumn to give new plants almost all year round. Look out for the cultivars 'Blush', the outer leaves of which are tinged with pink; 'Mini Green', a miniature crisphead, which can be set as close as 4½–5 in. (13–14 cm) apart; and

loose-leaf varieties such as frilly edged 'Fristina and claret-red 'Revolution'. Slugs and aphids are the main pests, and lettuces are also susceptible to downy mildew and grey mold.

**Oriental greens.** Fast-growing oriental greens respond well to the cut-and-come-again treatment both as seedlings and at the semi-mature stage. Their ultimate size is controlled by their spacing—the more space they have, the larger they will grow. These are cool-season crops, which tend to bolt in hot, dry weather, and they are best sown in mid- to late summer for autumn and winter harvest. They need fertile, moisture-retentive soil and full sun. They can either be sown directly into the container where they will germinate rapidly, or be raised in cell-pack trays and transplanted when they are large enough to handle. **Chinese cabbage** (*Brassica rapa* var. *pekinensis*) matures 8–10 weeks from sowing and is easy to grow in containers. It forms heads of bright green leaves, varying in shape from barrel-like to cylindrical. There are loose-leaf types that are less prone to bolting. **Mizuna greens** (*B. rapa* var. *nipposinica*) are a good, low-temperature crop. The deeply cut, dark green leaves have a fresh, crisp taste and can be eaten raw in salads, cooked with meat dishes, or pickled. Mizuna grows well between sweet corn as a cut-and-come-again crop. **Bok choy** (*B. rapa* var. *chinensis*) is an easy-to-grow vegetable for containers with bright green leaves that have prominent white veins. The height varies depending on the cultivar, and they can either be harvested young or thinned out and left to mature. The small, neat Shanghai bok choy is best suited to containers. **Spinach mustard** or komatsuna (*B. rapa* var. *perviridis*) is an exceptionally fast-growing plant, bearing large, bright green, sometimes red-tinged, leaves with a mild but distinct mustard flavor. Flea beetles and slugs are the main pests of all these plants.

**Radicchio.** A form of chicory, radicchio (*Cichorium intybus*) forms an attractive plant with glossy green leaves that may be tinged with bronze and red, the colors spreading and deepening as they mature to form crisp, succulent round heads. Radicchio is very cold tolerant and is the perfect winter crop. Sow seed outside in pots in early summer for late-summer picking or in late summer for a winter crop. 'Palla Rossa' produces tight heads of leaves that turn redder as the temperature drops; it can be grown for its leaves and hearts or forced for chicons (young white leaves). 'Rossa di Treviso' has red-and-green variegated leaves. 'Rossa di Verona' has deep red leaves that form tight heads; if you cut plants back in autumn and protect them with a cloche, radicchio plants will sometimes produce a second head in spring. Slugs may be a problem, but radicchio is usually trouble free.

**Salad burnet.** This easily grown, evergreen perennial herb (*Sanguisorba minor*) is completely hardy. Plants, which grow to 3 ft. (1 m) tall, have attractive, bright green leaves, divided into oval leaflets, and spikes of red flowers in summer. Sow seed in spring and grow in any well-drained soil in sun or partial shade. The leaves, which have a rather nutty flavor with a hint of cucumber, can be harvested at almost any time of the year and are particularly useful for winter salads. Slugs can be a problem, but salad burnet is otherwise trouble free.

**Salad leaves.** In addition to well-known lettuce, there is a huge and ever-expanding range of plants with interesting, often colorful, edible leaves that can be added to salads to give a variety of flavors. You can buy packets of seeds containing mixtures of edible leaves. Look for mixtures such as 'Saladini' and 'Mesclun' (misticanza) in seed catalogs. Sow seed outdoors in pots in early to mid-spring for summer cropping or in mid- to late summer for winter cropping under cover. These plants need fertile, well-drained but moisture-retentive soil. Water them regularly to prevent bolting. The group includes **Amaranths** (*Amaranthus* spp.), which are more often grown as ornamental plants, but some species and varieties, such as *Amaranthus tricolor*, have tasty leaves that are a worthy substitute for spinach. Some also produce nutritious edible seeds. Red amaranths have ornamental leaves tinted red or purple. **Corn salad**, also known as lamb's lettuce or mache (*Valerianella locusta*), has a low, carpeting habit, and is an ideal cool-weather salad green for relatively shallow containers and will provide a virtual year-round crop of small green leaves. Although it does not bolt easily, its flavur diminishes in warm weather. Corn salad has the most flavor when young, so make small successional sowings every couple of weeks from early spring. **Mustard leaves** (*Brassica hirta*) germinate and develop quickly and are an ideal cut-and-come-again crop. Sow seed thickly in spring or early summer and keep cool and well watered for a

Lettuce

Red amaranth

Radicchio

Variegated land cress

super-fast crop. Red-leaved cultivars are particularly attractive. There are green-, red- and golden-leaved cultivars of **orache** or mountain spinach (*Atriplex hortensis*) that tastes much like spinach. The colorful young leaves can be added to salads, but it is best to steam more mature leaves before eating. When left to grow, orache can reach 5 ft. (1.5 m) or more in height, so nip out the growing tips to encourage branching and use them in salads. Sow orache in late spring or early summer when all danger of frost has passed. **Para cress** or Brazil cress (*Acmella oleracea*) is an unusual but attractive trailing annual, bearing bronze-green new shoots and leaves, coupled with small, round, yellow-bronze flowers. It is easy to grow from seed. Add the young leaves and shoot tips to mixed salads for extra flavor. **Summer purslane** (*Portulaca oleracea*) is a fleshy-leaved salad plant, and the golden-leaved form, *P. oleracea* var. *aurea*, is particularly ornamental. The leaves can be picked 4–8 weeks after sowing. They have a sharp taste and are best used sparingly in salads or cooked. The stems and leaves can be pickled.

**Sorrel.** A hardy perennial, sorrel (*Rumex acetosa*) forms a rosette of basal leaves above which long stems with long-stalked leaves and spikes of small red flowers are borne, reaching 24 in. (60 cm) or more tall. There are several variants, of which blood-veined sorrel is the most decorative, with its deep green leaves prominently veined dark red. Sow seed in spring or autumn, spacing plants 12 in. (30 cm) apart, and remove the flower spikes to encourage leaf production. Grow in deep, slightly acid, well-drained soil in sun or partial shade. French or buckler-leaved sorrel (*R. scutatus*) is a compact, low-growing leafy green plant with a less pungent flavour that can be added to soups, salads and used as a seasoning for seafood, potato dishes, and rice. Apart from slugs, sorrel is trouble free.

**Spinach.** Spinach (*Spinacia oleracea*) is a highly nutritious, cool-weather crop, and it is often said to taste better after a frost. It is fast and easy to grow in containers and is particularly useful for sowing among slower-maturing crops because the spinach will be harvested long before the other crop matures. Sow seed outdoors in early to late spring, and in late summer and early autumn for a succession of plants. They need fertile, well-drained, alkaline soil. For the best flavor keep the leaves tender and hydrated by ensuring the soil is evenly moist. In hot weather spinach has a tendency to bolt, so plants should be harvested as soon as they show signs of doing so to save the crop. 'Teton' is a compact variety and 'Bordeaux' has attractive red stems. The main problems are slugs and downy mildew.

**Swiss chard.** Cultivars of Swiss chard (*Beta vulgaris* Cicla Group) are among the most colorful and striking of all leafy vegetables. They can be grown as cut-and-come-again crops but should be sown thinly because they do not grow well if overcrowded. Sow seed under cover in early spring or outdoors in mid-spring. They need fertile, well-drained, alkaline soil and must be watered regularly to prevent bolting (running to seed). Swiss chard, also known as silver chard and seakale beet, grows to about 18 in. (45 cm) tall and has attractive dark green leaves with fleshy white ribs; cultivars include 'Lucullus', 'Fordhook Giant', and 'White Silver'. Rhubarb chard has dark green, crinkled leaves and dark red stalks and veins; 'Feurio' is more bolt resistant than some. 'Bright Lights' has red, pink, yellow, orange, and white ribs. Perpetual spinach or spinach beet has small, dark green leaves borne over a long period; this is a good substitute for ordinary spinach although with a slightly coarser texture. Beet leaf miner is the main pest.

**Winter cress or land cress.** A good winter salad crop, winter cress (*Barbarea vulgaris*) has peppery-flavored leaves that both look and taste somewhat like watercress. The variegated form *B. vulgaris* 'Variegata' has leaves are splashed creamy yellow. Leaves can be harvested all year round, but plants are best covered with cloches to keep them in good condition through the winter. Plant in a container in fertile, well-drained soil in full sun or partial shade. Seed sown in mid- to late summer can be cropped from winter to spring. Water regularly to prevent plants from bolting. Flea beetles are the main pests.

# Edible roots and tubers

**Beets or beetroot.** Beets (*Beta vulgaris* subsp. *vulgaris*) are mostly grown for their edible roots, which are commonly globe-shaped, but sometimes cylindrical or tapered, but the leaves, especially when young, are also edible and make a tasty addition to salads. Sow seed in cell-pack trays under cover from late winter to early spring or outdoors in containers from early spring to mid-summer for a succession of plants. Grow beets in well-manured, well-drained soil, and in an open, sunny position. Water regularly to prevent the roots from turning woody and bitter. Most beet "seed" actually produces several seedlings, which makes thinning and spacing difficult. However, for a good crop from a small space, beets can be multi-seeded, which means growing 6–8 seedlings in a single pot and planting them together. As they grow they produce a clump of small but perfectly shaped roots. If you prefer to grow individual plants look for monogerm seed. There are numerous cultivars. 'Kestrel F1', 'Monaco', and 'Detroit 2—Little Ball' are suitable for growing as mini-beets, but 'Bull's Blood', which has dark red leaves, 'Chiogga', with its candy-striped roots, and 'Boltardy', with its dark red roots, are reliable and widely available. Apart from bolting in hot weather, beets are trouble free.

**Carrot.** Unless you are growing them in particularly deep containers, such as the drainage pipes in the Towering Thymes project (see pages 40–41), it is best to choose round or stump-rooted varieties of carrot (*Daucus carota* var. *sativa*) for a container because they do not require such a depth of growing mix. Carrots do not transplant well, so sow seed under cover in biodegradable pots or cell-pack trays in late winter or outdoors in containers in early spring. Carrot seeds are tiny, so are best sown in small pinches and thinned out to about 1 in. (2.5 cm) apart in order to allow the roots to develop. To avoid root disturbance, thin out by snipping off the unwanted seedlings at soil level rather than pulling them out. Make successional sowings every few weeks from early spring to late summer for a continuous supply of tender young roots. Carrots dislike heavy,

rich soils, preferring free-draining, sandy ones. 'Early French Frame' and 'Parmex' produce round roots, which are best eaten when they are the size of golf balls. 'Redcar' and 'Chantenay Red Cored' that are also ideal for containers develop short, stumpy roots. The most common pest is carrot fly. However, these fly close to the ground and are less likely to attack carrots raised above soil level in containers.

**Potato.** Early potatoes (*Solanum tuberosum*) are best suited to containers because they crop quickly and have less top growth than main crop types. Plant the tubers in late spring in as large and as deep a container you can find and can allocate space for, setting them about 4 in. (10 cm) apart on a 4–5 in. (10–12 cm) bed of all-purpose mix. Cover them with a 2–3 in. (5–8 cm) layer of mix. Shoots will emerge within a couple of weeks, and when they are about 6 in. (15 cm) high, add more mix, burying them halfway. Repeat this process a few times through the growing season as potato tubers grow from the part of the stem that is below soil level, and this will encourage them to crop well. Keep them well watered but not too wet, which encourages disease. When grown as "new" or salad potatoes, they can usually be harvested around two months or so from planting. Otherwise let them flower and allow the top-growth to wither before taking them out of the container. Choose cultivars such as 'Accent', 'Arran Pilot', and 'Swift'. Blight, which can devastate crops, is the main problem of potatoes have, but this affects plants in summer in periods of warm, wet weather and is unlikely to affect early potatoes grown in containers.

**Radishes.** Radishes (*Raphanus sativus*) are fast maturing and ideal for growing among other crops that take longer to develop. They will grow in sun or light shade, but when they are grown in warmer conditions the roots tend to have a stronger, more peppery taste. The roots are generally rounded and form just below soil level, so these are ideal crops for shallow containers. They can also be spaced fairly closely so it is possible to grow a good crop in a relatively small container. Radishes are best sown directly in a container every couple of

| Beets | Potatoes | Radishes | Carrots |

weeks from early spring to early autumn for a succession of crops, but they can also be started in cell-pack trays and transplanted when they are large enough. They do best in well-drained, fairly rich, alkaline soil. Many cultivars with roots of varying colors and shapes are available: 'Helro', 'Cherry Belle', and 'Sparkler' have round, red-skinned roots; and 'Pink Beauty' has round, pink-red roots. Long varieties such as 'French Breakfast' can also be grown in containers very successfully. Flea beetle and cabbage root fly can be problems, and radishes are also susceptible to clubroot.

**Turnips.** Most familiar as a large root vegetable, there are also numerous smaller cultivars of turnips (*Brassica rapa* Rapifera Group) that can be harvested when they are small and tender and used immediately. These turnips do not store well but are ideal as a side vegetable, steamed or sautéed, added to summer soups, or grated in salads. The leaves can also be cooked or, when young, eaten raw. The roots can be harvested when they are 1 in. (2.5 cm) across, so they can be sown fairly close together and gradually thinned out. Like radishes, they are best sown directly into the container, around other crops such as sweet corn or peas, but they can also be raised in cell-pack trays and later transplanted. They need fairly rich, well-drained soil and regular watering. 'Arcoat', a summer turnip, has red-topped, white roots. 'Tokyo Cross', also a summer crop, is a fast-growing cultivar, best sown from early summer to prevent bolting. Turnips are prone to many of the same pests and diseases as cabbages (see page 138). They are also susceptible to violet root rot and suffer from turnip gall weevils.

## Edible bulbs and stems

**Garlic.** Provided they are positioned in a warm spot and are watered regularly, garlic (*Allium sativum*) grows surprisingly well in containers. Garlic needs a long growing period for best results, and to maximize space while they are maturing, intersperse them with fast-growing salad leaf crops (see page 140). Plant individual cloves (pointed end up) in late autumn or, in mild areas, in late winter to early spring. They need free-draining, fertile, alkaline soil that must never dry out. The range of cultivars has increased in recent years. 'Cristo' produces large bulbs, whether it is sown in autumn or spring. Also suitable for autumn or spring planting are the strongly flavored 'Fleur de Lys' and 'White Pearl'. 'Long Keeper' does best from autumn planting, but 'Printanor' and the mild 'Sultop' are good choices for spring planting. Onion bulb fly and basal rot are the main problems.

**Kohlrabi.** The edible part of kohlrabi (*Brassica oleracea* Gonglyodes Group) is the swollen stem that develops just above soil level and tastes like cauliflower. They can be used steamed or boiled with other vegetables or grated raw in salads. Kohlrabi is best harvested when the roots are the size of billiard balls, 8–10 weeks from sowing, before they become tough and woody. Sow seed in cell-pack trays under cover from late winter or outdoors in containers from early spring, sowing at two-week intervals to give a succession of plants. Grow in well-drained, light soil in full sun, setting seedlings 8 in. (20 cm) apart. Among the best cultivars for growing in containers are 'Logo' and 'Rolando'. F1 hybrid 'Kolibri' is purple-skinned and 'Green Delicacy' is a pretty pale green. Although they are susceptible to the same pests and diseases as other *Brassicas*, it is usually harvested before it can succumb to them because kohlrabi is so quick growing.

**Leeks.** Leeks (*Allium ampeloprasum*) are generally thought of as staple plants in the vegetable plot, but they are one of the vegetables that can be grown successfully as mini- or baby vegetables. Sow seed directly in pots from early spring to early summer, thinning seedlings to ½ in. (1 cm) apart as they emerge. The plants will grow quickly as long as they are in fertile, well-drained soil and are watered regularly. Pick them when they are as thick as a pencil, pulling them in bunches. Grown in this way, leeks are an excellent substitute for spring onions and can be used in salads or braised. If you allow them to grow, they can be pulled when they are about ½ in. (1 cm) in diameter. 'King Richard' and 'Jolant' are the best cultivars to grow in this way. Leeks suffer from onion fly maggots and are susceptible to white rot and rust.

**Onions.** Traditionally grown onions (*Allium cepa*) are too large for most containers, but most cultivars can be harvested before they are fully mature. It is also possible to multi-sow onions, putting 6–8 seeds together in individual pots or cell-pack trays. Instead of thinning the plantlets, transplant the whole pot, setting the clumps about 6 in. (15 cm) apart. They will develop into small, perfectly round onions. Seed can be sown in cell-pack trays under cover from late winter or early spring and outside in containers from mid-spring. Sets (immature onions) can be planted where you want them to grow but generally become too large for most containers, although the closer you plant them the smaller they will grow. Onions need well-drained, alkaline soil in an open, sunny position. There are many cultivars, of which 'Shakespeare', 'Imai', and 'Shimonita' are particularly suitable for growing as mini-onions. The main pests are onion fly and onion thrips. Onions are also susceptible to several diseases, including onion neck rot and smut.

**Shallots.** Shallots (*Allium cepa* Aggregatum Group) have a milder, more delicate flavor than onions. When they are grown from sets they form multiple bulbs, but seed-grown plants produce single bulbs. Seed can be sown outdoors from early spring, while sets are usually planted from late winter. Seeds can be multi-sown, with 6–8 seeds to each pot and planted out in clumps. Shallots need the same conditions as onions (see above). Immature shallots can be harvested and used in the same ways as spring onions. 'Ambition' and 'Matador' are usually grown from seed; 'Delicato', 'Pikant', and 'Red Sun' are grown from sets. Shallots suffer from the same pests and diseases as onions.

## Podded vegetables

**Asparagus peas.** An unusual half-hardy annual is the asparagus pea (*Lotus tetragonolobus*), which bears small, winged (four-sided), edible pods containing smooth, brown seeds. The whole pods are usually picked when they are about 1 in. (2.5 cm) long and steamed and served with butter. The common name derives from the fact that they taste like asparagus. Sow seed in peat pots under cover in early spring or outdoors in late spring, after the last frost. The seeds develop into small bushes with trailing stems that reach 16 in. (40 cm) in length. Bright red flowers are borne in summer, and the pods follow the flowers, 8–10 weeks after sowing. These plants are trouble free.

**French beans.** One of the mainstays of the vegetable plot are French beans (*Phaseolus vulgaris*), which are increasingly included in borders and ornamental plantings because of their attractively colored flowers and fruit. Get plants off to an early start by sowing seed in biodegradable pots under cover in mid-spring; harden off and plant out only after the last frost. Alternatively, sow directly in pots in early summer. Plant into fertile, well-drained, alkaline soil and grow in full sun. There are several dwarf cultivars that are particularly suitable for containers, including 'Aramis', 'Arosa', 'Cropper Teepee', 'Ferrari', 'Maxi', 'Masai', 'Mont d'Or', 'Safari', and 'Sungold'.

| Kohlrabi | Shallots | Asparagus peas | Runner beans |

'Purple Teepee' and 'Golden Teepee' bear attractive purple and yellow pods, respectively. The main pests are bean seed fly, black bean aphids, and slugs.

**Hyacinth or dolichos beans.** Hyacinth beans (*Lablab purpureus*) are grown for the young pods and seeds (pulses), which can be used both fresh and dried. In temperate areas this tender perennial is grown as an annual, and it needs some support because it is a naturally climbing plant. Sow seed in pots under cover in spring and do not plant out until the temperature is about 64°F (18°C). The white or purple flowers are followed by green or purple pods, that reach 6 in. (15 cm) in length, which contain up to six seeds that may be white, cream, reddish, brown, or black. They are so decorative that they are often included in the flower section of seed catalogs. Although tender, these plants are trouble free.

**Peas.** There are few things that equal the flavor of freshly shelled peas (*Pisum sativum*), quickly cooked and served with butter and a little mint. As long as you have the space and choose cultivars carefully, it is possible to have peas from late spring to early autumn. However, if you are using a single cultivar for a container, make several sowings of seeds at two-week intervals, sowing under cover from early spring and outdoors as soon as the soil is warm and dry. (Peas will not germinate in cool, wet conditions.) Grow them in as deep a container as possible, using well-drained, alkaline soil. Water regularly but avoid wetting the soil too much. 'Feltham First' and 'Meteor' are compact varieties and 'Half Pint' is very dwarf.

'Sugar Dwarf Sweet Green' ('Norli') is a snow pea, and 'Sugar Rae'. 'Sugar Ben' and 'Sugar Gem' are compact sugar snap peas. Start harvesting pods from the bottom of the stem. Peas are susceptible to powdery mildew and are sometimes infested by pea moths that burrow into the peas inside the pods so the damage usually goes unnoticed until you start to shell the peas before cooking them.

**Runner beans.** Although they are really perennials, runner beans (*Phaseolus coccineus*) are grown as annuals in most temperate climates. They are mostly familiar in the garden when they are trained up wigwams, but dwarf cultivars are available and need no support. Sow seed under cover in late spring in biodegradable pots and harden them off for planting outside after the last frost. Runner beans need moisture-retentive, alkaline soil. To turn climbing runner beans into bushy, more manageable plants, pinch out the growing tips when they are around 12 in. (30 cm) high and remove any climbing shoots as they appear. The cultivars 'Kelvedon Marvel' and 'Scarlet Emperor', normally climbing forms, can be grown as bushes in this way. Among the true dwarf cultivars, which do not need staking, are the stringless 'Pickwick' and 'Hammond's Dwarf Scarlet', a widely grown, red-flowered cultivar, which will crop over a long period if the beans are picked regularly. The dwarf 'Hestia' has red and white flowers and is recommended for containers. Slugs and aphids are the main problems with runner beans, and in cold or dry conditions or when there are few flying pollinators failure to set pods can lead to a reduced crop.

| Eggplants | Gourds | Tomatoes | Chili peppers |

## Fruiting vegetables

**Eggplants (aubergines).** Among the most attractive of container-grown vegetables are eggplants (*Solanum melongena*), which bear fruit in a surprising range of shapes, colors and sizes. They do not grow well if there are too many other plants in the pot around them, but with a little coaxing they can usually be persuaded to give up space to low-growing crops, such as dwarf beans. Sow seed in early spring in a heated plant rack. Given plenty of heat, they will germinate well, but they resent root disturbance so are best sown in small individual pots. Grow them on in a warm, protected environment before hardening off and planting out after the last frost. Eggplants need fertile, well-drained, but moisture-retentive soil. Water regularly and apply a high-potash fertilizer as soon as fruits appear. Pick crops as they ripen to encourage the production of new fruits. 'Fairytale' has attractive striped fruits, and 'Billionaire' bears slender dark purple fruits and has purple-tinged foliage. The fruits of 'Crescent Moon' are long and white. Irregular and inadequate watering can cause blossom end rot, and the worst pests are aphids and, in dry weather, spider mites.

**Zucchini.** Traditionally, these half-hardy annuals grew too large for containers, but new cultivars of zucchini (*Cucurbita pepo*) have made it possible to get a worthwhile crop from pot-grown plants. Sow seed under cover in late spring, sowing two seeds to each biodegradablepot and removing the weaker seedling if both germinate. Plant out after the last frosts into fertile, moisture-retentive soil. These are "greedy" plants and need regular watering and feeding. Choose cultivars such as round, yellow-skinned 'One Ball' which is best harvested at tennis ball size, or 'Supremo', 'Patriot', and 'Bambino' which should be harvested when the fruits reach 6 in. (15 cm) in length. Powdery mildew affects plants in hot, dry weather, and zucchini are also susceptible to mosaic virus, which is spread by aphids. Slugs are the main pest.

**Cucumbers and gherkins.** To crop well, cucumbers and gherkins (*Cucumis sativus*) need a plentiful and consistent supply of fertilizer, water, and heat. They are climbing or trailing plants, and even those described as compact or semi-bush will still scramble around to some extent. They will require some form of support, such as a trellis or a pyramid, or they can be planted in a tall container and allowed to cascade over the sides. Sow seed into individual biodegradable pots, two seeds in each, in a heated plant rack in spring. Remove the weaker seedling if both germinate. To encourage sideshoots, pinch out the main growing tip once seven or eight leaves have formed. Plant in fertile, moisture-retentive soil after the last frost. They need a warm, sheltered spot in full sun. Although it is tempting to let cucumbers grow as large as possible, the smaller fruits are usually more succulent and have the best flavor. Pick regularly to encourage the formation of more fruits. Outdoor cultivars include 'Burpless Tasty Green'; 'Marketmore', which is resistant to virus diseases; and 'Bush Champion', which is a compact plant with dark green fruits. Older cultivars include 'Crystal Lemon' and 'Crystal Apple', which produce small, oval, pale yellow fruits that taste just like conventional cucumbers.

Gherkins are not small cucumbers, although they are grown in the same way. Look for cultivars 'Conda' and 'Venio'. Slugs and aphids are the main pests, and plants may suffer from powdery mildew in hot, dry conditions. However the main problem is cucumber mosaic virus, which is transmitted by aphids; always try to buy certified virus-free plants.

**Peppers and chilies.** Tender, annual, sweet or bell peppers (*Capsicum annuum* Grossum Group) and chili peppers (*Capsicum annuum* Longum Group) can be grown as compact, rather bushy plants that are ideal for containers in a sheltered, sunny part of the garden. Sow seed in a heated plant rack in early spring and plant outside only after the last frost in fertile, well-drained, but moisture-retentive soil. Like tomatoes, peppers and chilies need scheduled amounts of high-potash fertilizer and regular watering. There are dozens of sweet pepper cultivars, including 'Redskin', a compact form; 'Gypsy', which has pointed fruits that ripen from yellow-green through orange to red; and 'Marvras', which has dark purple fruits, ripening to red. Pick them when they are smooth and ripe and use within about ten days. Chili peppers range from the very hot 'Habañero' to the milder 'Hungarian Wax' (although this gets hotter as it ripens). 'Apache' is a particularly dwarf, red-fruited cultivar. Surplus chilies can be dried or frozen. The main problem is blossom end rot, the result of inadequate or irregular watering.

**Pumpkins, squashes, and gourds.** Pumpkins (*Cucurbita maxima*), squashes (*C. moschata*), and gourds (*C. pepo*) are easy to grow plants that have a reputation for being too large for containers. However, there is now such a range of shapes and sizes that it is possible to find cultivars that can be grown in a large pot. Sow seed under cover in early spring and harden the plantlets off before planting after the last frosts. They need fertile, well-drained, but moisture-retentive soil and a position in full sun. Summer squashes will bear fruit 7 or 8 weeks after planting out, while you can expect to harvest winter squashes and pumpkins 12 to 20 weeks after planting out. 'Jack Be Little' produces small orange pumpkins, about 4 in. (10 cm) across

that can be roasted. Among the smaller squashes are 'Sunburst' and 'Peter Pan'. The main problems are slugs, squash vine borer, and, in hot, dry weather, powdery mildew.

**Sweet corn.** Sweet corn (*Zea mays*) is not an obvious candidate for containers. However, a warm, sheltered, sunny spot and careful attention to watering and feeding can produce a worthwhile crop in a very small space. Sweet corn does not do well in cold, wet seasons. Sow seed under cover in biodegradable pots in mid-spring and plant out into warm, fertile, moisture-retentive soil after the last frosts. Choose mini-corn, such as 'Minisweet' or 'Minipop F1', which bear the small baby corns often included in stir-fries. Harvesting while young will help promote the production of new ears. It is possible to cram a lot of corn plants into a large container, but it is usually better to give the plants more space and include another, earlier maturing crop, such as dwarf beans or peas, at their feet. As well as the traditional yellow or white sweet corn cultivars, there are ornamental corns with colored cobs, most of which are better for drying and using for decoration rather than eaten. 'Red Strawberry' is suitable for making popcorn. The main problems are mice, birds, and slugs.

**Tomatoes.** Tomatoes (*Lycopersicon esculentum*) are ideal for containers and there are cultivars that are suitable for hanging baskets. Although they can be grown from seed sown in pots under cover in late winter, it is easier to buy plants and set them out after the last frost. They need a position in full sun and fertile, well-drained soil. Water and apply a high-potash fertilizer regularly throughout the growing season, although too much watering will impair the flavor. Cherry tomatoes, such as 'Cherry Belle', 'Gardener's Delight', 'Nectar', and 'Yellow Balconi', are ideal for containers, while 'Tumbling Tom Yellow' and 'Tumbling Tom Red' are a trailing form, perfect for a hanging basket. The main pests are aphids and whitefly. Inadequate watering causes blossom end rot (a sunken dark patch on the fruit), and outdoor tomatoes are susceptible to both early and late blight (see page 142).

# Fruits

Fruit trees, such as apples and pears, grown on dwarf rootstocks are ideal for planting in containers and will give a crop sufficient to warrant the space they will take up. As a bonus, they will supply an attractive, if fleeting, display of spring flowers.

Cane fruits, such as raspberries, are not well suited to growing in containers, but bush fruits can look very attractive in pots and give a worthwhile crop.

**Apples.** When you are choosing an apple tree (*Malus domestica*) to grow in a container make sure it is one that is grown on a dwarf rootstock such as M27, which will give a plant about 6 ft. (1.8 m) high. Use the largest container you can afford and have room for—a half-barrel, for example—and fill it with fertile, moisture-retentive but well-drained soil. Only a few apples are self-fertile, so check the pollination requirements of the cultivar before you buy. If you have space for only one apple, look for "family" trees that have three cultivars grafted onto the same rootstock. Also check to see whether you have chosen a spur-bearing or tip-bearing apple, which will affect the pruning. Make sure the container is in a sunny spot and water regularly so that the soil never dries out. Although you could grow some ornamental annuals in the same container as the tree during the first year, the tree will grow better in subsequent years if nothing competes with it for nutrients and moisture. Apple trees are susceptible to mildew, canker, rust, and scab and may be infested by apple sawfly maggots and codling moths, which make holes in the fruits, and by aphids and capsid bugs.

**Bananas.** Banana plants (*Musa* spp.) make striking ornamental plants for a sheltered patio or sunny corner, but they are not hardy and need to be moved to the protection of a heated greenhouse in winter. The large leaves are easily damaged by strong winds, and even in summer they need a sheltered position. Buy plants from a nursery or divide an established plant in the spring. Bananas need fertile, well-drained soil and a location in full sun. Fruits are most likely to be borne on *M. acuminata* 'Dwarf Cavendish', as long as winter temperatures do not fall below 59°F (15°C). It will eventually grow to 10 ft. (3 m) tall and across. When they are grown in greenhouses, bananas are susceptible to mealybugs and aphids.

**Blueberries:** Blueberries (*Vaccinium corymbosum*) are one of the best fruits to grow in containers because they need moist, acidic soil, with a pH of 4.0–5.0, which is rarely found in gardens. They are perfectly hardy deciduous bushes, although late frosts can kill the spring flowers. Always use rainwater for watering. Although blueberries are self-fertile, you get a better crop if you have space for two plants. Early cultivars include

**Apples**

**Blueberries**

**Cranberries**

**Mandarin oranges**

'Bluecrop', which bears large, well-flavored fruits that ripen by late summer, and 'Patriot' that has especially large fruits. Mid-season blueberries include the vigorous 'Berkeley', 'Herbert', 'Ivanhoe', and 'Goldtraube'. Late-season cultivars include 'Jersey' and 'Coville'. Prune to encourage the production of new branches because the fruits are borne on two- and three-year-old wood. Remove dead wood in winter as well as branches that are four years old. Blueberries rarely suffer from pests and diseases, although it may be necessary to net plants to protect the fruits from birds. Yellow leaves are a sign of iron deficiency or a too high soil pH.

**Cape gooseberries.** The Cape gooseberry (*Physalis peruviana*) is related to the ornamental Chinese lantern or bladder cherry (*P. alkekengi*), and its small yellow fruits are enclosed in similar papery calyxes. The tender perennials, which grow to about 3 ft. (1 m) tall, can be grown from spring-sown seed, but it is easier to plant roots. Grow in well-drained, fertile soil in full sun. There are several cultivars, including 'Goldenberry' and dwarf 'Little Lantern', both of which have large, golden-yellow fruits. The fruits can be eaten fresh but are more often used for jams and jellies. The plants are trouble free.

**Citrus.** Oranges (*Citrus aurantium*), lemons (*C. limon*) and other citrus fruit can be grown successfully in containers as long as they can be moved to a frost-free position in winter. They are spiny, evergreen shrubs, with glossy green leaves and fragrant, white flowers in spring. Plant in well-drained, fertile soil. The best-known lemon cultivar is 'Meyer', which is a compact form with round fruits. Citrus fruits that are grown in greenhouses are often infested with spider mite, whitefly, scale insects and mealybugs; plants grown outside sometimes suffer from root rot.

**Cranberries** Like blueberries, cranberries (*Vaccinium oxycoccos*) need moist, acidic soil, and they should be watered with rainwater. They are small, evergreen bushes, from 6 in. (15 cm) to 24 in. (60 cm) tall, with thin stems and small leaves. The round, red fruits, which should be picked before the first frost, are used for making cranberry jelly or sauce, the traditional accompaniment for turkey and game. The cultivar 'Olson's Honkers' bears large fruits, and 'Pilgrim' is a fast-growing form. Cranberries are rarely troubled by pests and diseases, but they do suffer from chlorosis if the soil pH is too high.

**Grapes.** A grape vine (*Vitis vinifera*) is not the easiest of fruits to grow in a container, but with perseverance you can encourage your plant to produce a worthwhile crop. A well-grown, well-pruned specimen allowed to grow on a short woody stem or "leg" as a standard will make a handsome addition to a sunny patio. Position the container near a warm wall to shelter the plant. The vine will crop best when it is grown in warm, dry, fairly poor soil, and when it has as much light, space, and air as possible. The fruits are borne on new growth, so after fruiting prune shoots back to encourage the formation of new ones for next year. Top-dress each spring with a seaweed fertilizer and give the vine a light liquid fertilizer every two or three weeks during the growing season. Strict, careful pruning will help keep it compact and productive. Molds and mildews can be a problem for grape vines, particularly in humid summers.

**Passion flowers.** The flowers of *Passiflora* spp. are followed by fruits that are usually edible if, as in the case of *P. caerulea* for instance, not always palatable. The species *P. edulis*, which is sometimes known as purple granadilla, produces fruits that can be used to make juice or to flavor ice cream. This is a tender plant, which needs a winter temperature no lower than 61°F (16°C), so make sure that the container is not so large that you cannot move it to a sheltered location in winter. These tendril climbing plants will need a trellis or other support. Plant them in fertile, moisture-retentive, but well-drained soil in full

| Pears | Passion fruit | Red currants | Strawberries |

sun. Hardier species, such as *P. caerulea*, may survive outdoors in winter in the south if they are in a sheltered position and protected from cold, drying winds.

**Pears.** If you grow a pear (*Pyrus communis*) in a container, make sure that it is growing on a dwarf rootstock such as Quince A, which will give plants to 12 ft. (3.6 m) high, or Quince C, which produces plants about 8 ft. (2.4 m) high. Only a few pear varieties are self-fertile or partially self-fertile, otherwise you will need to grow two compatible cultivars. Choose the largest possible container and position it in a sunny position, sheltered from strong, blustery winds. Use fertile, moisture-retentive, but well-drained soil. Pears need pruning to remove dead and damaged wood and to encourage a strong central leader to develop. They do not store as well as apples, and some cultivars are best eaten right from the tree.

**Red and white currants.** Red and white currants (*Ribes* spp.) are hardy deciduous shrubs, which are tolerant of a range of conditions. They grow well in any well-drained soil. They are self-fertile plants and form bushes about 4 ft. (1.2 m) high. The currants are borne on shoots that develop from the permanent framework of branches and will start cropping as soon as any branches are two years old. Redcurrant cultivars include 'Stanza' and 'Red Lake', and a reliable and popular whitecurrant is 'White Versailles'. All the currants are susceptible to mildew and may need netting to protect the currants from birds.

**Strawberries.** If you choose cultivars with care, it is possible to have strawberries (*Fragaria* x *ananassa*) from late spring to early autumn. Plant bare-rooted runners in summer or pot-grown plants in autumn, using fertile, well-drained soil in full sun. Because they are shallow-rooting plants, it can be difficult to plant them with other species in the same container, and they are usually mulched, traditionally with straw, to keep down weeds and to keep their fruits above the soil. Many cultivars are available: 'Earliglo' and 'Veestar' are early season plants; 'Catskill' and 'Redcoat' are mid-season cultivars; and 'Allstar' and 'Sparkle' are good, late-season plants. Among the perpetualy fruiting (remontant) plants are 'Autumn Beauty', 'Ogallala', and 'Tribute'. Mold can be a problem, and slugs and snails find strawberries irresistible, as do birds.

# Herbs

Many of the most popular and useful culinary herbs thrive in containers, and some, including rosemary and sage, are evergreen, providing a year-round display of aromatic leaves for cooking. When they are in pots herbs can be positioned where they are readily accessible—near the kitchen door, close to a path or on a windowsill—and they can be moved into a more sheltered positions for the winter months, even in a greenhouse, giving a supply of fresh young leaves for culinary use throughout the year.

**Basil.** This most flavorsome of herbs is a tender annual or short-lived perennial. Basil (*Ocimum basilicum*), which grows to about 20 in. (50 cm) tall, is cultivated for its aromatic leaves that are included in many vegetable dishes, especially those containing tomatoes, pasta sauces, and soups. Sow seed in pots under cover in spring and plant in fertile, well-drained soil after the last frost. Grow in full sun for best results. Pick the leaves as plants come into flower. There are many cultivars, including *O. basilicum* var. *purpurascens* 'Purple Ruffles' that has purplish black, crinkled leaves. Powdery mildew can be a problem in dry weather, and plants are sometimes infested with aphids.

**Black cumin.** Also called blackseed, is known as nutmeg flower and Roman coriander. Black cumin (*Nigella sativa*) is a hardy annual that grows to 12 in. (30 cm) high. It has finely divided leaves and small, white flowers in summer. These are followed by black seeds. Sow seed outdoors in autumn or spring in well-drained soil in full sun. The seeds can be used to flavor breads and pastries and are often included in curries and vegetable dishes. They can also be dried and used in infusions. These plants will self-seed and are trouble free.

**Borage.** The pretty, blue flowers of borage (*Borago officinalis*) are a popular addition to summer drinks and are often frozen into small ice cubes to add a splash of color. The cucumber-flavored leaves can also be added to drinks or in salads. Borage is a hardy annual, easily grown from seed sown in the spring. In the open garden it self-seeds freely, but in a container the flowerheads can be removed before they set seed. Plants grow to about 24 in. (60 cm) high and 18 in. (45 cm) across in any well-drained soil in full sun. Plants sometimes suffer from powdery mildew in hot, dry summers but are otherwise trouble free.

**Chamomile.** Roman chamomile (*Chamaemelum nobile*) is a hardy, evergreen perennial that grows to 6 in. (15 cm) high and 18 in. (45 cm) across. The white and yellow-centred, daisylike flowers are borne in summer and are used to make chamomile

**Chives**

**Lime mint**

**Oregano**

**Hyssop**

tea. Chamomile can be grown from seed sown in pots outdoors in spring, and established plants can be divided in spring. Grow in full sun in free-draining, fairly sandy soil. Infusions of the leaves are often used as a hair conditioner. The cultivar *C. nobile* 'Treneague', which does not bear flowers, is the plant to choose if you want a chamomile lawn. All these plants are trouble free.

**Chive and garlic chives.** The hollow, onion-flavored leaves of chives (*Allium schoenoprasum*) are frequently added to salads and egg dishes, and both the leaves and bulbs can be used in soups and sauces. Add the pretty flowers to salads for the distinctive taste of onion. Garlic or Chinese chives (*A. tuberosum*) is similar but has a stronger flavor and flat leaves. Sow seed of both these perennial plants outdoors in spring or divide established clumps in spring. They do best in well-drained, fertile soil in full sun. Water regularly during dry weather. Chives, which grow 12–18 in. (30–45 cm) high, bear pink, purplish, or sometimes white flowers in summer. Garlic chives, 10–20 in. (25–50 cm) high, have white flowers in late summer to autumn. Both are susceptible to the usual diseases of onions: white rot, downy mildew and onion fly.

**Coriander.** An aromatic hardy annual, coriander (*Coriandrum sativum*) that grows to 20–28 in. (50–70 cm) high, has bright green leaves and in summer pale purple flowers. These are followed by yellowish seeds, which can be dried. Sow seed in spring and grow plants in rich, well-drained soil. If you want to focus on the leaves, position coriander in partial shade; if you want to produce seeds, make sure plants are in full sun. The fresh leaves are used to flavor soups and sauces and can be used as a garnish. The dried seeds are included in curries and pickles. Coriander is largely trouble free.

**Cumin.** Cumin (*Cuminum cyminum*) is a half-hardy annual, growing only 12 in. (30 cm) high. It has divided, dark green leaves and flowers of white to pale pink clusters in midsummer. The flowers are followed by grayish seeds. The rather bitter

leaves are rarely eaten, but the seeds are an essential addition to curries and many Middle Eastern dishes. Sow seed in pots under cover in early spring or outdoors after the last frost. Grow in full sun in well-drained, rich soil. Cumin is trouble free.

**Dill.** A hardy annual, dill (*Anethum graveolens*) is grown for its feathery, aniseed-flavored leaves and the seeds that follow the clusters of yellow flowers. Sow seed outdoors in spring and grow in full sun in fertile, well-drained soil. Water regularly to prevent plants from bolting (setting seed). Some plants only grow to 2–3 ft. (60–90 cm) tall, but the dwarf cultivars 'Bouquet', to 24 in. (60 cm) tall, and 'Fernleaf', to 18 in. (45 cm) tall. They make pretty additions to summer containers. Use the leaves, fresh or dried, in preparing recipes and harvest and dry the seeds for infusions. Dill is a trouble-free herb to cultivate.

**Fennel.** A hardy perennial, fennel (*Foeniculum vulgare*) is a tall herb, growing to 6 ft. (1.8 m) or more. Sow seed in pots under cover in early spring or outdoors in late spring, spacing plants apart 18 in. (45 cm). Fennel needs deep, fertile, well-drained soil and a location in full sun. The feathery, dark green leaves have a distinct aniseed flavor, and in summer small, yellow flowers are borne in flat clusters and are followed by small seeds. The cultivar 'Purpureum' has bronze-purple leaves. The leaves and seeds are often used to flavor fish dishes, and the leaves make pretty garnishes. Florence fennel (*F. vulgare* var. *dulce*) is a biennial, grown for the bulbous stalk base, which is treated as a vegetable or included raw in salads. Fennel is usually trouble free, although aphids and slugs can be a problem.

**Fenugreek.** The half-hardy annual fenugreek (*Trigonella foenum-graecum*) can be easily grown from seed sown in pots outdoors in spring. Plants, which grow 20–24 in. (50–60 cm) high and to 18 in. (45 cm) across, need fairly deep, rich, free-draining soil and a location in full sun. The aromatic leaves, which can be used as a vegetable or dried for infusions, have three toothed

| Fennel | Lavender | Parsley | Pineapple mint |

leaflets. The yellow-white flowers are borne in late spring to summer and are followed by pods that contain yellowish seeds. Ground seeds are an ingredient in curries and pickles. These are trouble-free plants. If you have some seed left over and some spare ground in the vegetable plot, use fenugreek as a nitrogen-fixing green manure, sowing in late spring for digging in during late summer.

**French tarragon.** One of the traditional *fines herbes* is French tarragon (*Artemisia dracunculus*), which is a hardy perennial with a rather upright habit, 3–4 ft. (1–1.2 m) high, and has narrow, aniseed-flavored leaves. Small, yellow-green flowers appear in late summer but rarely set seed. Divide established plants in spring or autumn. Grow in full sun in well-drained, rich soil. Use the leaves to flavor egg and chicken dishes or add them to salads. Russian tarragon (*A. dracunculus* subsp. *dracunculoides*) is hardier and often sets seeds but has a less refined flavor than the species. French tarragon is susceptible to rust.

**Hyssop.** A semievergreen, hardy, shrubby perennial, hyssop (*Hyssopus officinalis*) has aromatic leaves and spikes of purple-blue flowers in late summer. There are variants with white and pink flowers. Plants grow to 24 in. (60 cm) high but tend to spread to about 3 ft. (1 m). Sow seed in autumn and keep in a cold frame until spring, when plants should be moved to well-drained, fertile, alkaline soil and a location in full sun. The leaves have quite a strong flavor and should be used sparingly in meat dishes. Plants are trouble free.

**Lavender.** There are dozens of cultivars of lavender (*Lavandula* spp.), with flowers in every possible shade of blue, pink, and purple as well as white. All have the familar wonderful, unmistakable fragrance and small, grayish leaves. Lavenders are evergreen shrubs, and *L. angustifolia* and its cultivars are hardy. Most other lavenders require some protection in winter. They need well-drained soil and a position in full sun. Some lavenders can grow large and quite leggy, so for containers look out for more compact cultivars, such as *L. angustifolia* 'Lavenite Petite', 'Princess Blue', or *L.* Bella Series in a range of colors. Use the fresh flowers in ice cream or vinegar or crystallize them to decorate cakes and puddings. Lavenders grown in well-drained soil in containers are usually trouble free.

**Lemon grass.** A familiar ingredient in many Southeast Asian fish and meat dishes, lemon grass (*Cymbopogon citratus*) is a tender perennial. It forms clumps of linear leaves and can grow to 5 ft. (1.5 m) high. In cold areas it can be kept in a heated greenhouse in winter and moved outdoors in summer. Established plants can be divided in spring. As well as being a useful culinary ingredient, the lemon-flavored leaves can be used fresh to make tisanes. Plants are trouble free.

**Lemon verbena.** Lemon verbena (*Aloysia triphylla*) is potentially a quite large, deciduous shrub, growing to 10 ft. (3 m) high and across if left unpruned. In late summer it bears little, pale lilac flowers in panicles. This herb is not reliably hardy and needs the protection of a sheltered patio or a deep mulch over the roots in winter. Lemon verbena is usually propagated from cuttings,

| Purple basil | Golden curly marjoram | Sage | Lemon-variegated thyme |

so look for plants in garden centers. Prune the plants in spring, cutting back the main stem to 12 in. (30 cm). Lemon verbena does best in full sun in any well-drained soil. Pick the aromatic leaves to use fresh in tisanes and salads or you can dry them for a delicious, citrus-flavored tea. As long as they do not get too cold in winter, lemon verbena plants are trouble free.

**Marjoram and oregano.** The perennials and subshrubs in the genus *Origanum* have aromatic leaves and spikes of pink flowers in summer. Sweet marjoram (*O. majorana*) is a half-hardy subshrub that grows to 24 in. (60 cm) high, which is often treated as an annual in temperate areas. Oregano (*O. vulgare*) is a hardy perennial that grows to 18–36 in. (45–90 cm) high. There are many cultivars, with different leaf and flower colors. Sow seed of sweet marjoram in pots under cover in spring and plant after the last frost. Sow oregano seed in autumn or spring or divide established plants in spring. The fresh leaves of both marjoram and oregano are widely used in Italian and Greek cuisines, and the dried leaves are suitable for infusions. Aphids are sometimes troublesome.

**Mint.** Mints (*Mentha* spp.) are among the easiest herbs to grow, and they are particularly well suited to growing in containers that restrict their very invasive roots. They are hardy perennials, which can be grown from seed sown in spring. Established plants can be divided in spring or autumn. They do best in moisture-retentive but not too rich soil and prefer a position in full sun. Most have pinkish or purplish flowers, borne in spikes in summer above the aromatic leaves, which

may be variegated. They range in habit from the creeping Corsican mint (*M. requienii*) which grows about ⅓ in. (1 cm) high, to the vigorous "eau-de-cologne" mint (*M. x piperata* f. *citrata*), which can grow to about 20 in. (50 cm) high and spread to 3 ft. (1 m). Of all the available types, Moroccan mint (*Mentha spicata* var. *crispa* 'Moroccan') is perhaps the best culinary mint and one of the best for general all-around use. Rust and, in dry weather, powdery mildew may cause problems.

**Parsley.** One of the most widely used of culinary herbs is parsley (*Petroselinum crispum*). Its bright green leaves are used to flavor soups, stews, butters, and savory dishes of all kinds and as a garnish. Flat-leaf parsley has a stronger flavor than the curly-leaved form. Parsley is a hardy biennial that grows to 24 in. (60 cm) high. Sow seed outdoors from spring onward for a succession of plants and water regularly until germination, which should be from 4–6 weeks after sowing. Transplant to 6 in. (15 cm) apart in rich, moisture-retentive but well-drained soil. Grow in full sun or partial shade. Carrot fly larvae and celery fly larvae can damage roots and leaves, respectively. Hamburg parsley (*P. crispum* var. *tuberosum*) is grown for its parsnip-like roots, which are harvested in autumn and early winter. Sow seed outdoors in alkaline, fertile soil in partial shade; plants mature in about 30 weeks and have a better flavor if left in the ground rather than being lifted and stored. Parsnip canker is the main problem.

**Rosemary.** Rosemary (*Rosmarinus officinalis*) is an evergreen shrub, with aromatic leaves and, in summer, blue, pink, or white flowers. Although it is not absolutely hardy, the species and most of the numerous cultivars will withstand frosts for short periods. Although rosemary can be grown from spring-sown seed, it is easier to buy plants and transfer them to well-drained, soil and a location in full sun. The species can grow to 5 ft. (1.5 m) tall, and the other most widely available cultivar, 'Miss Jessopp's Upright', is also tall growing. The smaller 'Severn Sea', to 3 ft. (1 m) tall, or even the low-growing (but less hardy), 'Prostratus' that grows to 6 in. (15 cm) high are better for containers. The leaves are a traditional accompaniment for lamb but can also be added to cakes and fruit preserves or used to infuse olive oil. Plants are usually trouble free.

**Sage.** This large genus, *Salvia*, includes ornamental bedding annuals as well as perennial and shrubby culinary herbs. Common sage (*S. officinalis*) is a hardy, shrubby, evergreen perennial that grows to 32 in. (80 cm) high, with velvety, gray-green leaves and purple-blue, pink, or white flowers. Numerous cultivars have been developed, including 'Tricolor', which has gray-green leaves with cream and pink margins, and the compact 'Kew Gold', which has green-flecked, golden-yellow leaves. The species (*S. officinalis*) can be grown from spring-sown seed but the cultivars should be grown from cuttings taken in summer or purchased as plants. Grow them in well-drained soil in full sun. The leaves can be used to make tea or to flavor meat dishes and cheeses. These sages can be affected by leafhoppers.

**Summer savory.** A hardy annual, summer savory (*Satureja hortensis*), which grows to 10–15 in. (25–38 cm) tall, has narrow green leaves and whorls of lilac to white or purple flowers in summer. Sow seed in pots under cover in late winter or outdoors in spring and grow plants in well-drained, fertile, alkaline soil in full sun. The leaves, a traditional ingredient in *herbes de Provence*, can be used fresh in meat dishes and to flavor stuffings. Winter savory (*S. montana*) is a hardy dwarf subshrub, with pink-purple flowers. Use the leaves of winter savory in the same way as those of summer savory. Both plants are trouble free.

**Sweet bay.** A large evergreen shrub or tree, bay (*Laurus nobilis*) has aromatic, rather leathery leaves and, in spring, clusters of small, yellowish flowers that are followed (on female plants) by black berries. In open ground bay trees can grow to 40 ft. (12 m) tall, but container-grown plants can be pruned to keep them in proportion to the pot. They need deep, fertile, well-drained soil and some protection from cold, drying winds. They do best in full sun. The leaves are a familiar addition to marinades, soups, and stews and are also a traditional ingredient in bouquet garni. Scale insect can be troublesome, and bays are sometimes affected by powdery mildew and leaf spot.

**Thyme.** The large genus, *Thymus*, includes several small, evergreen perennials and subshrubs that often do better in the free-draining conditions that can be provided in a container than in the open garden. Garden or common thyme (*T. vulgaris*), a hardy subshrub that grows to 12 in. (30 cm) tall and has aromatic, gray-green leaves and purple to white flowers in late spring and early summer; the cultivar 'Silver Posie' has white-edged leaves and *T. citriodorus* 'Golden King' that grows to 10 in. (25 cm) tall has yellow-edged leaves. Thymes are readily raised from summer cuttings, but it is usually easier to buy plants of the cultivar of your choice. Plant in well-drained, neutral to alkaline soil in full sun. The small leaves of thyme are included in bouquet garni and as an ingredient in many classic French dishes. The leaves are also used in stuffings, casseroles, and marinades. The plants are trouble free.

# Edible flowers

**Agastaches.** There are numerous species and cultivars of agastache. The most commonly used culinary variety is anise hyssop (*A. foeniculum*), which will grow 3–5 ft. (1–1.5 m) tall and bear spikes of small, purplish-blue flowers. All agastaches require well-drained soil and a sunny location, flowering from mid-summer to early autumn. Species can be raised from seed sown in pots under cover in spring, while cultivars should be propagated by division in spring. These are sturdy, largely trouble-free plants, which sometimes suffer from powdery mildew in dry weather.

**Cornflowers.** A hardy annual, cornflower (*Centaurea cyanus*) has dark blue flowers from late spring to mid-summer. Plants grow to 32 in. (80 cm) tall and have gray-green leaves. Smaller cultivars, better suited to containers, include the Baby Series, which grow to 12 in. (30 cm) tall and have blue, pink, or white flowers. Sow seed in pots outdoors in autumn or spring and plant seedlings in well-drained soil in full sun. The flowers are used fresh in salads or dried and included in potpourri blends. Although largely trouble free, cornflowers are susceptible to powdery mildew in hot, dry weather.

**Clove pinks.** Clove pink or gillyflower (*Dianthus caryophyllus*)—from which carnations are descended —is a hardy, evergreen perennial that grows to 20 in. (50 cm) tall, with gray-green leaves and pink to purple, clove-scented flowers in summer. Sow seed in pots under cover in spring or buy plants of named cultivars and plant them in fertile, well-drained soil in full sun. Deadhead regularly to encourage new flowers. The fresh flowers can be added to salads, although they are mostly used to flavor syrups and liqueurs. Powdery mildew and root rot can be problems.

**Daylily.** Hardy herbaceous perennials, daylilies (*Hemerocallis* spp. and cultivars) form clumps of narrow strap-shaped leaves and strong stems bearing a profusion of lilylike blooms in summer. Colors range from deep orange-red, through yellow and pink, to creamy white and each flower lasts just a day. Daylilies thrive in moisture-retentive but free-draining soil in full sun or partial shade and are best divided in spring every three years. The buds and the petals are edible, having a sweet flavor reminiscent of water chestnuts and a crunchy lettuce-like texture. Like many edible flowers, they should be eaten in moderation. Use in salads and stir-fries, and for garnishing. There are thousands of named varieties, ranging in height from 12 in. (30 cm) to 4 ft. (1.2 m). Daylilies are generally trouble free, although slugs and snails are atttracted to the tender new shoots in spring.

**Pot marigolds.** Fast-growing, hardy annuals, pot or English marigolds (*Calendula officinalis*) have aromatic leaves and single or double daisylike flowers in shades of yellow, orange, cream, and gold in summer and autumn. There are numerous cultivars, the names often indicating the flower color: 'Orange King', 'Lemon Queen', 'Pink Surprise', and 'Greenheart Orange'. Most are 18–24 in. (45–60 cm) high. They grow easily from spring- or autumn-sown seed and will tolerate fairly poor soil as long as it is well drained. Deadheading regularly will encourage new blooms. The petals can be used (instead of saffron) to color rice, and they are also tasty in butters, cheeses, and cakes, or sprinkled over salads. Plants are susceptible to aphids and powdery mildew. Most grow 18–24 in. (45–60 cm) high, but there are also several dwarfer, more compact forms.

**Primroses.** The most welcome of spring flowers are primroses (*Primula vulgaris*), which bear pale yellow fragrant flowers in spring above rosettes of bright green leaves. They are hardy perennials, growing to 8 in. (20 cm) high. Sow seed in late winter or early spring and grow in partial shade in rich, well-drained but moisture-retentive soil. Divide established plants regularly to maintain their vigor. The flowers and leaves can be added to salads, and the flowers are pretty garnishes for puddings with delicate flavors. Plants are susceptible to gray mold and slugs.

| Violas | Nasturtium | Pot marigolds | Cornflowers |

**Nasturtiums.** The vividly colored flowers of nasturtiums (*Tropaeolum majus*) are a frequent addition to salads, but the peppery leaves can also be eaten in salads, and the seeds can be pickled and used as a substitute for capers. There are many hybrids, which can be easily grown from seed sown in pots outdoors in spring or started under glass for earlier flowers. These annuals are naturally climbing or trailing plants, but there are an increasing number of dwarf or compact cultivars available. Nasturtiums do best in full sun and moisture-retentive but free-draining soil; if it is too rich, however, plants will produce leaves at the expense of flowers. Look out for compact varieties, such as 'Empress of India', which gets to 12 in. (30 cm) tall and has scarlet flowers; or plants in the Tom Thumb Series, which have bright yellow, orange, red, and salmon-pink blooms. Blackfly and cabbage white butterfly caterpillars can devastate nasturtiums. Be vigilant and remove the pests by hand.

**Scented-leaved pelargoniums.** This group of tender, shrubby, evergreen perennials has highly aromatic foliage, which releases its strong fragrance when the plants are brushed. They are quite different from other members of the genus *Pelargonium*, such as the ivy-leaved and zonal forms, which are popular bedding plants. Scented-leaved pelargoniums have small single flowers that may be pink, purple, or white, and mid-green leaves, which may be variegated with gold or silver. Buy plants from a good nursery or garden center and plant them in well-drained, fertile, neutral to alkaline soil. Deadhead to encourage new flowers and lift before the first frost to overwinter in a dry, frost-free greenhouse. The leaves of lemon-scented pelargonium

(*P. citronellum*), lemon-scented pelargonium (*P. crispum*) and apple-scented pelargonium (*P. odoratissimum*) can be used to make tea, but these plants are mostly grown for their fragrant oils. Plants are susceptible to gray mold and aphids.

**Sunflowers.** Most sunflowers (*Helianthus annuus*) are too tall for containers, some growing to 10 ft. (3 m) or more, but some shorter cultivars of these hardy annuals have been developed, including the compact 'Teddy Bear' that grows to 3 ft. (90 cm) high, and 'Big Smile', to 16 in. (40 cm) high. Sow seed in pots outdoors in spring and grow in fertile, moisture-retentive but well-drained soil in full sun. While they are still green, the flower buds are edible and can be fried in butter, while the seeds can be eaten raw or roasted. In hot, dry summers powdery mildew can be a problem. Plants should be protected from slugs and snails.

**Violas and pansies.** The annuals and perennials in the genus (*Viola*) have been widely hybridized to produce numerous cultivars. If you require only a few plants it is most sensible to buy plantlets, although seed can be sown in pots in late winter for early spring and summer flowers or in summer for winter flowers. Grow them in moisture-retentive but well-drained, fertile soil in sun or partial shade. The dainty sweet violet (*V. odorata*) bears fragrant, dark purple or white flowers from late winter to early spring. These flowers are often used as a garnish for desserts or fresh in salads, and they can be crystallized or frosted (with egg white and sugar) to decorate cakes. Slugs and snails can be a problem, as can powdery mildew in dry weather.

# Index

**A**
acid soil mixes 15
*Agastache*
  growing instructions 156
  projects 78
*Ajuga reptans* 120
amaranth 141
American cress 68
annual flowers 12
aphids 12, 27
apples
  growing instructions 21, 148
  project 112
  recipe 112
arugula
  growing instructions 140
  projects 74, 98, 107
  recipe 64
asparagus peas
  growing instructions 144
  project 86

**B**
backgrounds, siting containers 11
banana plants
  growing instructions 25, 148
  project 124
basil
  growing instructions 154
  project 98
bay, sweet
  growing instructions 21, 25, 153
  project 102
beans
  sowing 19
  see also specific plant name
beets
  growing instructions 18, 142
  projects 37, 64
  recipe 64
*Begonia* 112
biological pest control 27–29
black-eyed Susan 38
blackfly 27
blight 28
blueberries
  growing instructions 25, 148–9
  project 114
  recipe 114
bok choy
  growing instructions 140
  project 44
  recipe 44
borage
  growing instructions 152
  project 50
borecole 139
botrytis 28
brassicas 19, 27
  see also cabbages

**C**
cabbages
  growing instructions 25, 138
  project 100
  recipe 100
*Calendula officinalis*
  growing instructions 156
  projects 67, 68
*Calibrachoa* 94
Cape gooseberries
  growing instructions 149
  project 134
*Carex comans* 78
carrots
  growing instructions 18, 142
  project 37
  recipes 37, 91, 124
caterpillars 27
cauliflower
  growing instructions 138
  project 73
  recipe 73
cell-pack trays, sowing seeds 19
*Centaurea cyanus*
  growing instructions 12, 156
  project 67
ceramic pots 13
chamomile
  growing instructions 152
  project 126
  recipe 126
chard
  growing instructions 138
  projects 73, 81, 92
  recipe 92
chemical pest control 29
cherries 21
chicken
  recipes 52, 94, 104
chili peppers
  growing instructions 147
  projects 82, 104
  recipes 82, 104
Chinese cabbage
  growing instructions 139
  project 108
Chinese chives 60, 107
chives 151
choosing containers 13–14
citrus fruits 26, 149
clary, annual 88
climbing plants 12, 21
clove pinks 156
coir, soil-less mixes 15
companion planting 12
containers
  choosing 13–14
  concrete 14
  grouping 11
  siting 11
coriander
  growing instructions 152
  projects 60, 78, 82, 107
corn salad 141
cornflowers
  growing instructions 12,156
  projects 67
cranberries
  growing instructions 25, 149
  project 114

**D**
daylilies 156
deadheading 21
*Dianthus*
  growing instructions 156
  project 122
dill
  growing instructions 151
  projects 52, 60
diseases 20, 28–9
  see also specific disease names
division 18
dolichos beans 145
drainage 16
drip systems 23
dwarf beans
  growing instructions 21, 144–5
  projects 46, 63, 77, 86,

**E**
edible flowers 67, 156  7
  see also specific plant names
eggplants
  growing instructions 146
  projects 77, 88
  recipes 77, 88
endive 138–9
ericaceous soil mixes 15

**F**
F1 hybrids 18
feeding plants 26
fennel
  growing instructions 18, 152–3
  project 97
  recipe 97
fennel, bronze 97
fenugreek 155
fertilizers 17, 26,
fiberglass containers 14
fish, recipes 78, 102
flowers
  deadheading 21
  edible 156–7
French beans
  growing instructions 144–5
  projects 63, 86
  recipe 86
fruit 12, 21, 148–50
  see also specific plant names

**G**
gages 21
garlic 143
garlic chives
  growing instructions 151
  projects 60, 107
geranium
  growing instructions 102, 157
  project 117
germination, seeds 18, 19
gherkins 146–7
glazed ceramic pots 13
gooseberries 18

**H**
hanging baskets, planting 17
*Helianthus annuus*
  growing instructions 156
  project 67
*Hemerocallis* 156
herbs 18, 21, 151–5
  see also specific plant names
hops 130
hyacinth beans 145
hybrids, F1 18
hygiene 16, 20, 29
hyssop
  growing instructions 153
  projects 78, 84

**I**
improvised containers 14
insecticides 29
insects 12
*Ipomoea*
  growing instructions 12
  project 70
irrigation systems 23

**K**
kale
  growing instructions 139
  projects 60, 73, 100
kohl rabi
  growing instructions 143–4
  project 91
  recipe 91

**L**
land cress
  growing instructions 141
  project 68
lavender
  growing instructions 18, 25, 153
  project 67
leaf beet
  growing instructions 138
  projects 60, 81, 92
leaf miners 27
leafhoppers 27
leeks
  growing instructions 144
  project 64
lemon balm 18
lemon grass
  growing instructions 152
  project 82
lemon verbena
  growing instructions 151
  project 126

**G** (cont.)
gourds
  growing instructions 12, 21, 147
  project 130
grape vines
  growing instructions 149
  project 120
  recipe 120
gray mold 28
greenfly 27
grit
  horticultural 15, 25
grouping containers 11

lemons
    growing instructions 149
    project 117
    recipes 50, 117, 120
lettuces
    growing instructions 19, 25,
        139
    growing with flowers 43, 49,
        64
    projects 37, 43, 49
    recipes 43, 49
lime-hating plants 15
liners, hanging baskets 17
lobelia 49
Lotus maculates x berthelottii
    104

**M**
marigolds
    French marigolds 12, 29
    growing instructions 12, 29, 156
    pot marigolds 67, 68, 156
    projects 67, 68
marjoram
    growing instructions 154
    projects 74, 97
melons 18
metal containers 13, 14
mildew, powdery 28
mint
    growing instructions 10, 18, 153
    projects 81, 84
    recipes 81, 84, 91
mizuna greens
    growing instructions 139–40
    project 44
morning glory
    growing instructions 12
    project 70
mulching 25
mustard
    growing instructions 141
    project 44

**N**
nasturtiums
    growing instructions 157
    projects 60, 67, 94
nectarines 21
nitrogen 26

**O**
olive trees
    growing instructions 25
    project 98
onions
    growing instructions 25, 144
    project 54
    recipe 78
orache 141
oranges 149
oregano
    growing instructions 154
    projects 74, 97
organic gardening 29
Oriental greens 139–40
ornamental plants, mixing with
    edible plants 12
overwatering 23

**P**
para cress
    growing instructions 141
    projects 97
parrot's beak 104
parsley
    growing instructions 18, 154
    projects 38, 52, 60, 68, 84,
        107
passion flowers
    growing instructions 21, 149–50
    projects 134
passion fruit 149–50
    recipes 112, 134
pasta, recipe 58
peaches 21
pears
    growing instructions 21, 150
    project 133
    recipes 54, 108, 133
peas
    growing instructions 19, 145
    project 33
peat 15
Pelargonium
    growing instructions 102, 157
    projects 117
pennyroyal 81
peppermint
    growing instructions 153
    projects 84, 126
peppers
    growing instructions 18, 19,
        147
    projects 82, 94
    recipes 64, 94
perennial flowers 12
perlite 15
pests 12, 20, 27–9
    see also specific pest names
pinks 156
pizza, recipes 34, 74
planting
    hanging basket 17
    pot 16
plastic pots 13
Plecostachys serpyllifolia 64
plums 21
poisonous plants 12
pollination 12
popcorn 129
potash 26
potatoes
    growing instructions 142
    project 84
    recipe 84
potting mixes
    additives 15
    choosing 15
    mulching 25,
    planting containers 16
    sowing seeds 19
powdery mildew 28
primroses 157
propagation 18–19
pruning 20–1
pumpkin 147
purslane 141

**R**

radicchio
    growing instructions 140
    projects 92, 108, 133
    recipe 108
radishes 142–3
red cabbage
    project 100
    recipe 37
red currants
    growing instructions 150
    project 122
rhubarb chard 139
risotto, recipe 70
roof gardens 13
rosemary
    growing instructions 18,
        154–5
    project 102
runner beans
    growing instructions 12, 21,
        145
    projects 46, 70, 77
    recipe 46
rust 28–9

**S**
sage 88, 155
salad, recipes 37, 43, 52, 54, 64,
    67, 86, 91, 97, 98, 107
salad burnet
    growing instructions 140
    project 50
salad leaves
    growing instructions 18, 26,
        140–1
    project 34
Salvia elegans 117
Salvia viridis 88
savory
    growing instructions 155
    projects 78, 82
seafood, recipe 44
seeds, sowing 18–19
self-watering containers 24
shallots 25, 144
siting containers 11
slugs 25, 27, 29
snails 25, 27
soil-based mixes 15
soil-less mixes 15
sorrel
    growing instructions 141
    projects 68
sowing seeds 18–19
spider mite 27
spinach
    growing instructions 141
    project 54
    recipe 54
spinach mustard 140
squashes
    growing instructions 18, 147
    project 130
    recipe 130
sterilizing equipment 20
Stipa tenuissima 78
stir-fry, recipes 33, 46
stone containers 14
stone fruits 21
stoneware pots 13

strawberries
    growing instructions 18, 150
    projects 50, 60, 118, 129
    recipes 50, 129
sunflowers
    growing instructions 156
    projects 46, 67
supports 21
Sutera cordata 64
sweet peas 33
sweet corn
    growing instructions 147
    projects 63, 129
    recipe 63

**T**
tarragon, French
    growing instructions 152
    project 52
    recipe 52
terra-cotta pots 13
terrazzo containers 14
thyme
    growing instructions 18, 155
    projects 40, 52, 60, 78, 84, 91
    recipe 40
tomatoes
    fertilizers 26
    growing instructions 147
    in hanging baskets 38
    pests 12
    pinching out sideshoots 20
    projects 58, 74, 133
    recipes 38, 74, 77, 81, 82, 86
    sowing 18, 19
    supports 21
topiary, trimming 21
training plants 21
tulips 43
turnips 143

**V**
vegetables 138–47
    see also specific plant names
Verbena 64
vermiculite 15
vine weevils 27, 29
violas
    growing instructions 157
    projects 43, 60, 67

**W**
water-retaining granules 15, 23
watering 19, 22–4
waterlogging 23
wetting agents 23
white currants 150
whitefly 12, 28, 29
winter cress 141
wooden containers 14
woodlice 28

**Z**
zucchini
    growing instructions 146
    projects 58, 124
    recipe 124

# Useful resources

### In the United States

**W. Atlee Burpee & Co.**
Toll-free: (800) 888-1447
www.burpee.com
*A mail-order supplier offering a large variety of vegetable, herb, and flower seeds, as well as a wide selection of gardening supplies.*

**Fedco Seeds**
Phone: (207) 873-7333
www.fedcoseeds.com
*A co-op garden supplier of cold-hardy plant varieties and gardening supplies.*

**Gardener's Supply Company**
Toll-free: (888) 833-1412
www.gardeners.com
*Offers a range of supplies, including seed-starting materials; containers, including self-watering containers; flower supports and more.*

**Peaceful Valley Farm Supply**
Toll-free: (888) 784-1722
www.groworganic.com
*Carries seeds and nursery stock; specializes in organic supplies.*

**White Flower Farm**
Toll-free: (800) 503-9624
www.whiteflowerfarm.com
*A mail-order nursery providing a wide range of ornamental and edible plants, plus tools and supplies.*

### In Canada

**Dominion Seed House**
Toll-free: (800) 784-3037
www.dominion-seed-house.com
*Supplier of herb, flower, and vegetable seeds as well as plant bulbs and accessories.*

**Halifax Seed Company**
Phone: (902) 454-7456
www.shop2.itnweb.com/halifaxseed
*Canada's oldest continuously operating seed company; supplies seeds and other gardening products.*

**Ontario Seed Company**
Phone: (519) 886-0557
www.oscseeds.com
*Supplier of high-quality flower, vegetable, and herb seeds.*

**Sheridan Nurseries**
Phone: (416) 798-7970
www.sheridannurseries.com
*Full-service chain of nurseries with 10 stores in Ontario.*

**Stokes Vegetable Garden Seeds**
Phone: (905) 688-4300
www.stokesseeds.com
*Supplier of seeds and accessories for home and commercial gardeners.*

**Vesey's Seeds**
Phone: (902) 368-7333
www.veseys.com
*Supplier of seeds, plants, bulbs, and gardening products.*

**West Coast Seeds**
Phone: (604) 952-8820
www.westcoastseeds.com
*Certified handler and supplier of organic seeds.*

# Acknowledgments

With endless thanks to my mum, Carol, for her unfailing love and support; to Judy Holbrook and Andy Luft for their invaluable help, advice, and friendship; and to all at Hamlyn, especially Sarah Ford and Clare Churly, for their patience, expertise, and guidance. My gratitude also goes to those individuals and companies who have helped along the way. Lastl, but certainly not least, thank you, Freia, for remaining calm and for producing such gorgeous images.